T0369357

TRANSFORMATIVE LEADERSHIP

CREATING AND SUSTAINING A THRIVING SCHOOL CULTURE

SHANA BURNETT, Ed.D

TRANSFORMATIVE LEADERSHIP
CREATING AND SUSTAINING A THRIVING SCHOOL CULTURE

iUniverse books may be ordered through booksellers or by contacting:

iUniverse
1663 Liberty Drive
Bloomington, IN 47403
www.iuniverse.com
844-349-9409

ISBN: 978-1-6632-6190-8 (sc)
ISBN: 978-1-6632-6189-2 (e)

Library of Congress Control Number: 2024907157

Print information available on the last page.

iUniverse rev. date: 08/19/2024

DEDICATION

In humble tribute to the torchbearers of knowledge, I dedicate this book to the dedicated educators whose passion lights the way for the next generation amidst the ever-shifting landscapes of our world. Your commitment to nurturing young minds is a beacon of inspiration, and this work is dedicated to all those who tirelessly sow the seeds of wisdom in the fertile minds of the future.

To my parents, whose love and guidance transcend the boundaries of time and space, I dedicate these pages with profound gratitude. Your enduring presence from another realm constantly reminds me of the values and principles that shape my journey.

In reverence to the divine orchestrator of our existence, I extend my heartfelt dedication to God, the creator of all things. It is with deep gratitude that I acknowledge the profound purpose bestowed upon me in this life, a purpose intertwined with the noble pursuit of transformative leadership in the realm of education.

May this book stand as a testament to the dedication of educators, the enduring influence of parental love, and the divine guidance that fuels the meaningful purpose we find in shaping the minds of the future.

"It's the going through that helps you get through." - Dr. Shana Burnett

CONTENTS

FOREWORD

MAYOR RAS J. BARAKA

In the vast world of education, where leadership plays a crucial role, school leaders are seen as the foundation of a thriving and nurturing learning environment. The decisions, initiatives, and commitments made by these leaders greatly influence the culture of our schools, creating spaces that either promote intellectual growth or risk becoming chaotic and dissatisfying.

Dr. Shana Burnett, an esteemed educator, takes us on an enlightening journey through the history of education. Her focus on the important role played by exceptional leaders in bringing about cultural change within our schools is both timely and profound. As a former teacher, principal, and current mayor of New Jersey's largest city, I understand the impact that leadership can have on the overall culture of an educational institution.

My own experience in education began as a teacher in a public school in my hometown. Throughout those years, I witnessed firsthand the transformative power of leadership. During this time, I crossed paths with Dr. Burnett, who served as a teacher coach. Her unwavering commitment to staff and students left a lasting impression on me, and we worked together under the guidance of a trailblazing principal who embodied passionate leadership.

Dr. Burnett's career, rooted in a commitment to her hometown, reflects the essence of dedication to the city where she was born and raised. Her classroom experiences and leadership positions provide deep insights into the dynamics of cultural transformation and the crucial importance of transformational leadership.

In this groundbreaking work, Dr. Burnett explores the historical developments in education and delves into the transformative potential that exceptional leaders bring. With a particular focus on urban schools, this research-rich journey addresses a significant gap by offering invaluable insights into the complex connections between leadership styles and school culture.

As readers explore the pages of this book, they will encounter real-life examples and cutting-edge leadership theories. Dr. Burnett skillfully navigates the challenges and successes of educational leadership, emphasizing the profound impact that leaders have on the lives of students and staff.

This work goes beyond exploration; it serves as a call to action for every school leader, teacher, and administrator. May the insights within these pages inspire and empower those who shape the educational landscapes of our communities. Dr. Shana Burnett's dedication to this field is a guiding light, urging us all to embrace the transformative power of leadership in pursuing excellence in education.

INTRODUCTION

Have you ever considered the nuanced effects of diverse leadership styles on educational institutions? In the intricate complexity of education, the threads of leadership profoundly impact a school's culture. Within the walls of every school, whether urban or rural, lies the potential for fostering either a sanctuary of growth and harmony or a breeding ground for discord and disarray. This book embarks on a journey to explore the historical underpinnings of education and the pivotal role extraordinary leaders play in sculpting cultural metamorphosis.

The landscape of educational research often overlooks the intricate dance between leadership styles and school culture, especially within the dynamic context of urban schools. Yet, within these bustling environments, the need for understanding and harnessing the power of leadership becomes most acute. Amidst this scarcity of scholarly exploration, it is imperative to delve into this terrain to catalyze profound transformations in school culture.

Drawing upon rich experiences spanning over a quarter-century within the realm of public education, I have traversed the corridors of numerous schools, assuming diverse roles from educator to principal. Each role offered a unique vantage point, allowing me to observe the kaleidoscope of leadership styles and their profound impact on the cultural ethos of learning communities.

These immersive experiences ignited a genuine curiosity, propelling me towards pursuing deeper insights into the nexus of leadership and cultural transformation. As an ardent advocate for educational advancement, my journey led me to embark on rigorous research endeavors during my doctoral studies, focused on unraveling the mysteries of effective leadership and its ramifications on student achievement.

I sought to unearth the underlying dynamics through a meticulous blend of quantitative analysis and qualitative inquiry. Interviews with visionary school leaders in the bustling urban landscape of New Jersey provided invaluable glimpses into the inner workings of transformative leadership. Anchored by the seminal work of Bolman and Deal (1991) and their four-frame leadership model - encompassing the structural, human resource, political, and symbolic dimensions - my research endeavors illuminated the profound interplay between leadership style and school culture.

The findings of this inquiry serve as beacon lights in the labyrinth of educational leadership, revealing that the contours of school culture and student achievement are intricately intertwined with the leadership ethos permeating its corridors. Principals wielding structural or analytical leadership styles emerged as architects of positive cultural metamorphosis, fostering environments conducive to academic excellence.

However, the landscape is nuanced, as evidenced by the varied outcomes associated with human resource-oriented leadership approaches. Amidst this complexity, the imperative for data-informed decision-making resonates resoundingly, underscoring the pivotal role of leadership in narrowing achievement gaps and nurturing a culture of collective growth.

As you embark on this exploration, may the insights gleaned from these pages serve as a compass, guiding your reflections on leadership and its profound implications for school culture. I earnestly hope this journey will empower you to assess and refine your leadership practices, fostering environments where every individual can flourish and thrive.

CHAPTER 1

SCHOOL HISTORY

How does your leadership contribute to shaping the history of education within your school district? What deliberate actions are you taking to instigate profound changes in the school culture that leave a lasting impact on students, educators, and the wider community?

Having dedicated over twenty-five years to the field of education, I've been an active participant in the evolution of school culture and leadership within our district. My journey into education, particularly in an urban setting, was fueled by a profound commitment born from the challenges I witnessed firsthand as a child. However, my experiences have taught me that effecting meaningful change in schools necessitates collaborative effort.

As a seasoned educator, I've seen the ebb and flow of educational trends and policies, but what remains constant is the need for visionary leadership and a collective drive for improvement. In my role, I strive to be a catalyst for positive change, working alongside fellow educators, administrators, and community stakeholders to shape the education trajectory within our district.

Recognizing that transformation requires more than just individual effort, I am committed to fostering a culture of collaboration and innovation. Through deliberate actions and strategic initiatives, I aim to instigate profound changes that not only enhance the educational experience for our students but also empower educators and engage the wider community.

From implementing inclusive teaching practices to promoting professional development opportunities, my leadership endeavors are centered on creating an environment where every school community member feels valued, supported, and inspired to excel. By nurturing a culture of continuous improvement and embracing diversity, we can leave a lasting impact that transcends generations, shaping the history of education in our district for years to come.

I have firsthand experience of how leadership influences school and district events. A leader must support the school culture to make a significant difference in school transformation.

Educational leadership is more critical now than ever. In a landscape marked by unprecedented challenges and rapid transformations, effective leadership within our schools is paramount. This necessity becomes even more apparent when compared to dictator leadership at the national level. While dictatorship embodies centralized control and authoritarian decision-making, reminiscent of top-down management approaches, educational leadership aligns more closely with the principles of democracy.

As someone who deeply values the tenets of democracy and inclusivity, I've often found striking parallels between the democratic process and effective educational leadership. Just as democracy empowers individuals to participate in governance and decision-making, educational leadership empowers stakeholders within schools—students, parents, teachers, and administrators—to actively engage in shaping the direction and priorities of their educational communities.

In contrast to the autocratic tendencies often associated with dictatorial regimes, educational leadership promotes a culture of empowerment, collaboration, and accountability. Rather than imposing mandates from above, educational leaders work collaboratively with stakeholders to identify needs, set goals, and develop strategies that reflect the unique context of their schools and communities.

Drawing from my own experiences, I've witnessed firsthand the transformative power of inclusive and democratic leadership within educational settings. By fostering an environment where every voice is heard and valued, educational leaders not only cultivate a sense of ownership and investment among stakeholders but also inspire a shared commitment to collective growth and success.

In essence, while dictatorship represents a departure from democratic values and principles, educational leadership embodies the ideals of democracy in action. By championing inclusivity, transparency, and shared decision-making, educational leaders create environments where every member of the school community has the opportunity to thrive and contribute to the greater good.

Moreover, despite limited research availability on leadership styles and their influence on school culture, especially within urban schools, delving into this topic is crucial for effecting significant changes in school culture. As mentioned in the introduction, while much of the cited research in this book may be ten years or older, its value remains steadfast in understanding how different leadership styles contribute to transforming school culture and ultimately improving student achievement.

As I reflect on the district where I have dedicated significant time, I am struck by parallels that echo the intricate urban landscape portrayed in "The Wire" by David Simon. This sprawling district, classified as Abbott district schools in New Jersey, presents a vivid tableau of inequality across its four wards. Each ward serves as a microcosm, starkly highlighting the disparities in educational resources, facilities, administrative leadership, and overall atmosphere experienced by different socioeconomic strata. Much like the nuanced societal dynamics depicted in "The Wire," these disparities underscore systemic challenges that urgently demand comprehensive reform. Addressing the root causes of inequality is imperative to ensure equitable access to education for all students. This introspection compels us to confront the harsh realities of societal stratification and recommit to transformative action.

I grew up in the central and southern area of an urban city in New Jersey, and my parents chose to send me to private schools because they believed the public schools in our community did not meet the required standards.

This experience sparked a strong desire to become the best educator in my community and truly make a positive impact. I pursued a career in teaching because I wanted to ensure that learning could be enjoyable for students. Additionally, I became involved in coaching to support teachers in the classroom. I took on leadership roles to assist families, educators, and children through community partnerships, intending to provide the highest quality education for our young people. During my time as a school leader, I realized that one of the main challenges faced by schools was the burdensome bureaucracy that arose from a top-down management structure.

In my extensive observation of our school district, I meticulously tracked its evolution from locally managed to state-controlled and eventually back to local management amidst fluctuating leadership. This turbulent journey, characterized by shifting governance structures and leadership transitions, has provided me with unique insights into the complex dynamics of educational administration.

Initially, the district operated under local management with a sense of autonomy and community connection. Decisions were made with a keen understanding of local needs and priorities, fostering a sense of ownership among stakeholders. However, as challenges mounted and systemic issues persisted, the state intervened, assuming control of the district to implement reforms and address the underlying issues.

The period of state control brought about significant changes as external authorities implemented top-down strategies to improve student outcomes. While these interventions were well-intentioned, they often needed a more nuanced understanding of local contexts and cultures, leading to resistance and friction within the community. Moreover, frequent turnover in state-appointed leadership further destabilized the district, creating a sense of uncertainty and disarray.

Despite the efforts made during the New Jersey Department of Education state takeover, the district continued to grapple with persistent challenges that impeded student achievement. Issues such as inadequate resources, socioeconomic disparities, and systemic inequities remained deeply entrenched, thwarting attempts at meaningful progress. As a result, student performance stagnated, with minimal improvement observed over time.

Eventually, the district transitioned back to local management, signaling a return to community-driven decision-making and governance. While this shift was met with cautious optimism, it also brought to the forefront the daunting task of addressing longstanding issues that had been exacerbated during the period of state control. Leadership changes accompanied this transition as new administrators sought to navigate the complex educational reform and revitalization landscape.

Despite the renewed sense of local control, the district faced formidable challenges that demanded innovative solutions and sustained stakeholder commitment. Addressing these issues requires a collaborative and holistic approach to understanding the multifaceted factors influencing student achievement. Through concerted efforts to foster a culture of excellence, equity, and inclusivity, the district could overcome its longstanding obstacles and truly empower every student to thrive.

One positive change that impressed me throughout these transitions was the emergence of charter schools. This movement gave families the choice of selecting a different type of school. After closely collaborating with the administrators of some of the higher-performing charter schools, I witnessed how their leadership and school culture differed from those in traditional public schools. I became intrigued by the contrast in leadership styles and school culture despite both types of schools serving students from the same demographics. I observed how charter schools achieved significantly higher student success levels than traditional public schools in my district. School administrators at the charter schools had the freedom to make decisions that aligned with their unique school culture. Principals and school leaders should have the independence to govern their schools in a way that supports and maintains the school's culture instead of having restrictive leadership that impedes progress.

Reflecting on the past to understand the significance of school reform and its importance becomes apparent. The US Department of Education assigned the State Educational Agency (SEA) the responsibility of categorizing schools into three groups: Reward, Focus, or Priority. This initiative emerged as a response to the significant number of underperforming schools and low proficiency rates across school districts. The No Child Left Behind Act (NCLB), enacted in 2001, holds school districts accountable for student academic achievement.

In New Jersey, the designated Abbott district schools were classified as Reward, Focus, or Priority by the NJ Department of Education (NJDOE) in 2012. The NJDOE defines reward schools for high-performances based on the designation of adequate yearly progress (AYP). Focus schools have significant achievement gaps between subgroups, while Priority schools are among the lowest 5 % in student achievement based on AYP. According to the NJDOE 2012 report, there were 112 Reward schools, 183 Focus schools, and 75 Priority schools. This book will explore how leaders influence school culture and student achievement.

Priority schools, identified as the lowest performing, must adopt district-mandated programs to improve student performance. The American Recovery and Reinvestment Act of 2009 (ARRA) introduced the Race to the Top (RTT) grant to aid struggling schools. The RTT grant focuses on funding reforms that improve data collection and usage, enhance teacher performance, and upgrade curriculum to turn failing schools around. Regional Achievement Center (RAC) teams were established to support Focus and Priority schools, which the NJ Department of Education identified. Priority schools are those with low achievement rates, and if they continue to underperform despite support, they may face closure or be reclassified as Renew schools. Renewing schools requires vital personnel changes in administrative leadership and instructional staff. The underlying belief behind the restructuring efforts is that renewed leadership will improve student achievement. However, the empirical evidence for the differences between Priority and Renew schools' leadership philosophies has yet to be substantiated.

As I delve into the intricate dynamics of educational leadership and cultural transformation within schools, it's impossible to ignore the profound impact that effective leadership approaches can have on shaping the educational landscape. This book meticulously explores four key pillars of school culture:

- staff motivation
- professional development
- parental involvement
- student achievement.

Each of these components serves as a cornerstone, influencing the overall educational environment and setting the stage for meaningful change.

Remarkably, New Jersey emerges as a beacon of educational excellence, solidifying its position within the top 10% nationally for student proficiency in reading, a testament unveiled through the meticulous analysis of the 2022 National Assessment of Educational Progress (NAEP) among fourth- and eighth-grade students (NJDOE, 2022). However, this commendable achievement is juxtaposed against the stark reality of persistent disparities entrenched within the educational fabric of the state, a poignant narrative underscored most notably within the intricate landscape of its urban districts.

These urban enclaves stand as stark reminders of the immense challenges we still face in our quest for educational equity and excellence. Despite the progress we've made, there's no denying the systemic barriers that continue to hinder progress and perpetuate inequality.

In unpacking the nexus of leadership approaches and cultural transformation, it's imperative to confront the complexities inherent in our educational systems. By delving into each of the four areas of school culture, we aim to shed light on the nuanced dynamics at play and provide actionable insights for fostering positive change.

Yet, at the heart of it all lies the essence of leadership—the driving force behind every initiative, every decision, and every transformational endeavor. It's through visionary, inclusive, and collaborative leadership that we can navigate these challenges and steer our educational institutions toward a brighter future.

In harnessing the power of effective leadership approaches, we empower educators, administrators, and policymakers to effect meaningful change and drive continuous improvement. By embracing equity, promoting excellence, and fostering a culture of inclusivity, we can pave the way for a more equitable, empowering, and enriching educational experience for all students, regardless of their background or circumstance.

Student performance is assessed based on established criteria for student proficiency rates using state school report card data. The research focuses on the leadership philosophy and administrative style of elementary school principals from Renew and Priority schools. The Bolman and Deal (1991) leadership-style framework survey analyzes the principals' leadership style, determining the dominant style among symbolic, human resource, political, and structural. Principal interviews revolve around their teaching and leadership background and their views on the culture within their schools. These interviews discuss staff motivation, professional development, parental involvement, and student achievement. The principals' school achievement is compared based on data gathered from the NJDOE school report card, and a correlation is made between leadership style and school culture.

My findings unequivocally affirm the prevailing consensus in historical and contemporary educational literature through meticulous research and analysis: school leadership is the linchpin for a school's success or failure. Central to this assertion is the recognition that the effectiveness of a principal's leadership approach wields a profound influence on every facet of a school's operation, from its organizational climate to its academic outcomes.

Indeed, the spectrum of leadership approaches adopted by principals encompasses diverse styles, strategies, and philosophies, each bearing unique implications for cultivating school culture and advancing student achievement. Whether characterized by an emphasis on instructional leadership, transformative leadership, or distributed leadership, the approach adopted by a principal exerts a discernible ripple effect throughout the entire school community.

In essence, the leadership ethos cultivated by a principal sets the tone for the prevailing school culture, shaping staff and students' attitudes, behaviors, and aspirations. Principals who espouse a visionary, inclusive leadership style tend to foster an environment of trust, collaboration, and innovation, engendering a sense of collective purpose and efficacy within the school community. Conversely, principals who adopt a more authoritarian or transactional approach may inadvertently cultivate a climate of disengagement, distrust, and stagnation, ultimately impeding achieving academic goals and aspirations.

Moreover, the impact of principals' leadership approaches extends beyond the confines of the administrative domain, permeating into the very fabric of instructional practices and student experiences within the classroom. Principals who prioritize instructional leadership actively engage in curriculum development, instructional coaching, and pedagogical innovation, empowering teachers to excel in their craft and students to thrive in their learning endeavors. Conversely, principals who adopt a laissez-faire or hands-off approach to instructional leadership risk perpetuating mediocrity and complacency, compromising the quality and equity of education provided to students.

My research underscores the profound significance of school leadership in shaping the trajectory of educational excellence and equity. By recognizing the pivotal role of principals in cultivating a positive school culture and fostering student achievement, educational stakeholders are empowered to enact meaningful reforms and initiatives to nurture exemplary leadership practices that empower all students to succeed.

After researching and drawing upon my personal experiences, I understand leadership is crucial in enhancing student achievement. Michael Fullan (2001) states, "I know of no improving school that does not have a principal who is good at leading improvement." Effective schools have strong leadership, as identified in Sammons et al.'s (1995) study, which outlined eleven critical factors for effective schools, with professional leadership being discussed first. The study examined how leaders promote student achievement by influencing school and staff culture. All of the studies within this research literature agree that "outstanding leaders tend to be proactive." Sammons et al. (1995) also found that effective leadership was achieved through a shared approach involving all stakeholders in improving school culture.

The belief underlying the district's educational restructuring efforts is that Renewed leadership should lead to greater student achievement. However, the empirical evidence for differences in leadership philosophies between Priority and Renew schools is yet to be substantiated, despite several states implementing these strategies without measurable improvement in student achievement. Carter and Edmonds (2000) identified strong principal leadership as essential to successful high-poverty schools. They defined *successful urban schools* as those where principals could use their resources as they saw fit, established a culture of achievement, and employed highly skilled teachers who brought out the best in the faculty.

According to the NJDOE, Priority schools receive intervention and support from the district to assist them in achieving success, with principal leadership playing a critical role in turning around these schools. This is viewed as a last attempt to achieve different academic results with the existing teaching staff. Once a school is declared a Renew school, the changes are considered more radical. This label signifies that all previous measures must achieve the intended academic progress. The entire school leadership, teaching staff, and non-instructional staff are transferred to other locations, and a new administrator is assigned to lead the school. The administrator has the authority to choose the instructional and non-instructional staff. The qualifications for staff positions are based on New Jersey state certification guidelines for leadership and teaching staff.

Financial concerns often arise when considering our children's education. Barker (2018) underscores the importance of allocating additional resources to support educational institutions in his review of fair funding in education. Increasing funds for urban districts may not lead to better schools if the money is not used effectively. Additionally, school reform is acknowledged as essential for school improvement, with school leaders entrusted to demonstrate progress despite internal and external challenges.

In New Jersey, substantial reforms have been implemented, with the state taking control of its largest districts, which include Jersey City, Paterson, Newark, and Camden. The objective of this initiative is to enhance academic performance. New Jersey's most comprehensive reform policy resulted in the state taking over its four largest districts:

Jersey City in 1989 (which regained local control in 2020 and 2021), Paterson in 1991 (which regained local control in 2021), Newark in 1995 (which regained local control in 2018), and Camden in 2013 (which is currently under state control). Despite three of the mentioned districts no longer being under state control, there is still a significant amount of work to be done in reforming school culture to promote student achievement effectively.

Evolution of Educational Reform

What is your understanding of school reforms and the belief that they should be connected to a school's unique culture for the school community to thrive?

I have had numerous experiences serving as a public school educator in various roles. These experiences have allowed me to become part of different school communities in urban districts. Working independently has allowed me to see firsthand different leadership styles and the dynamics of different school cultures. Working with different administrators has given me insight into how these leadership styles can affect the learning environment. There has been a lot of debate about educational reform, especially concerning leadership and its effect on the educational system.

Over the past two decades, the education landscape has undergone a seismic shift characterized by the dynamic interaction between traditional public schools and charter schools within urban districts. This transformation has reshaped the educational ecosystem, fundamentally reevaluating how stakeholders perceive and engage with concepts like school quality, effectiveness, and accountability.

At the heart of this ongoing conversation lies the pivotal role of principal leadership, which has emerged as a linchpin for driving school success and shaping student outcomes in today's educational milieu. As traditional public and charter schools vie for prominence within urban districts, principals are the chief architects of their institutions' vision, culture, and instructional approaches. They wield significant influence over the trajectory of educational excellence and equity within their schools.

In this evolving landscape, principals serve as both stewards and innovators tasked with navigating the complexities of educational policy, fostering collaborative partnerships, and inspiring meaningful change within their school communities. Their leadership is instrumental in cultivating a culture of continuous improvement, fostering an environment where all students can thrive academically, socially, and emotionally.

As the educational landscape continues to evolve, the role of principals remains central to driving positive outcomes for students and advancing the broader goals of academic equity and excellence. Their leadership not only shapes the immediate experiences of students and educators but also leaves a lasting legacy that reverberates throughout the community and beyond.

In the competitive arena of urban education, principals are tasked with navigating many challenges and opportunities, from resource allocation and stakeholder engagement to curriculum design and instructional innovation. Principals who demonstrate visionary leadership are set to cultivate a culture of excellence, inclusivity, and ongoing improvement within their schools.

Moreover, as urban districts grapple with equity, access, and social justice issues, principals play a pivotal role in fostering environments that prioritize every student's holistic development and well-being. Principals who champion equity-centered leadership practices actively strive to dismantle systemic barriers and disparities, empower marginalized communities, and ensure that all students have equitable access to high-quality education.

Principal leadership catalyzes transformative change and collective action in the ongoing school quality discourse. Principals who adopt a collaborative, data-informed approach to leadership are better equipped to leverage their school communities' diverse talents and perspectives, driving meaningful progress and educational excellence.

However, more research is needed to compare leadership styles and school culture in Priority and Renew schools. It is often assumed that if there is a new administrator, there will be a significant difference in leadership. However, this has not been empirically investigated, nor have principals in these specific schools been trained by the NJDOE to address the challenges of improving them. Davis (2010) argued that for a school to be successful, the principal needs help to make all the decisions. Other stakeholders must work together with the principal to ensure a successful transformation.

Influential leaders take full responsibility for the success or failure of the schools they lead. Bolman and Deal's (2003) four-framework approach to leadership styles examines how leaders lead. These frames can overlap depending on how individuals perceive their environments and organizational culture. Of the four frames outlined by Bolman and Deal (1991), the structural frame is the most commonly used leadership style, followed by the human resource and political frames. The symbolic frame is rarely seen, but a Deal and Peterson (1990) study evaluated its importance in shaping school culture. The researchers focused on five studies of symbolic leadership strategies. Two of the schools studied were similar to this research because they were urban schools within a large district. An intriguing element across all the research, including this study, is the inclusion of the community in shared decision-making processes. Additionally, each study showcased a clear vision for their schools, demonstrated by their capacity to "read their school's culture and articulate a shared destiny."

According to the survey results presented in this study, a significant concern for urban school leaders is the need for more autonomy. The survey, sponsored by the US Department of Education, revealed that 34% of principals identified allocating funds as a moderate or severe obstacle to improving their schools. Additionally, 84% of urban principals expressed a desire for increased autonomy to achieve better results for their schools. Throughout all the research conducted by Deal and Peterson (1990), one emerging theme is the understanding among school leaders of the importance of school culture. A leader placed within a school must have a vision, understand the school's history, and be a good fit for the culture.

Notes

Workbook - Chapter One - School History

This workbook section for Chapter One is designed to help educational leaders reflect deeply on their contributions, deliberate actions, and understanding of school reforms. My goal is to encourage you to take practical steps that drive positive changes in your educational communities. By thoughtfully considering these aspects, you can better shape a thriving school culture and make a lasting impact on students, educators, and the wider community.

Shaping Educational History Through Leadership

- *Question 1:* How does your leadership contribute to shaping the history of education within your school district?

____

____

____

____

- *Reflection:* Reflect on your leadership journey and how your initiatives have influenced the educational landscape.

____

____

____

____

- *Action Step:* Document two key initiatives or programs you have led that have made a significant impact on your school district. Describe the outcomes and how they have shaped the district's educational history.

____

____

____

____

Instigating Profound Changes in School Culture

- *Question 2:* What deliberate actions are you taking to instigate profound changes in the school culture that leave a lasting impact on students, educators, and the wider community?

____

____

____

____

- *Reflection:* Consider the strategies and actions you have implemented to drive cultural change.

____

____

____

____

- *Action Step:* Develop a detailed plan outlining three specific actions you are taking to transform your school's culture. Include timelines, expected outcomes, and methods for evaluating success. Ensure these actions are sustainable and leave a lasting legacy.

____

____

____

____

Understanding and Implementing School Reforms

- *Question 3:* What is your understanding of school reforms and the belief that they should be connected to a school's unique culture for the school community to thrive?

____

____

____

____

- *Reflection:* Reflect on your knowledge of school reforms and their significance in your school's context.

____

____

____

____

- *Action Step:* Write a brief essay (300-500 words) on the importance of aligning school reforms with the unique culture of your school. Provide examples from your experience where this alignment has led to positive outcomes. Discuss the challenges and benefits of this approach.

____

____

____

____

Summary of Chapter One Insights

- *Reflection:* Summarize your key insights and takeaways from Chapter One in a concise paragraph.

____

____

____

____

- *Action Step:* Identify one new strategy you will implement based on what you have learned in this chapter. Describe how you will measure its effectiveness and the impact it aims to achieve.

____

____

____

____

CHAPTER 2

TYPES OF LEADERSHIP STYLES

How does your awareness of your leadership style influence the culture within your school community? What deliberate actions are you taking to ensure that your leadership style fosters a positive and inclusive environment for all stakeholders?

The opportunities I've had while working under different administrators have allowed me to gain insight into different leadership styles and how these styles can bring about cultural changes in learning environments. These experiences have given me a deep understanding of the dynamics of cultural transformation and the importance of transformational leadership. Therefore, it was easy for me to conduct research in these areas. As someone dedicated to professional and personal growth, I was always looking for innovative ways to improve education for children. I explored various research on how to train staff and parents to implement effective methods that promote academic growth for all students in all content areas.

According to the four-framework approach proposed by Bolman and Deal in 2003, leaders can be categorized into four groups. These categories can overlap and intersect with leadership styles that are associated with decision-making. The survey I used was based on these four frameworks. Researchers such as Leithwood et al. (2012) used different terms to describe leadership characteristics, such as transactional, transformational, and servant leadership. The dominant leadership style of each principal was identified, examined, and compared to their school culture based on their perceptions. These four frameworks include

1. structural
2. human resources
3. political
4. symbolic.

Structural Style

The structural leadership style focuses on productivity and clarity and emphasizes that classrooms and schools function most effectively when goals and roles are clearly defined. Leaders employing this style leverage authority, policies, rules, and informal strategies to coordinate the efforts of individuals and groups within the educational environment. Key to this approach is the emphasis on accountability and the establishment of measurable standards, guiding structural leaders' rational and analytical approach.

These leaders are often viewed as social architects, meticulously designing and orchestrating the organizational structure to achieve desired outcomes. Their leadership marks a systematic consideration of various elements, including structure, strategy, environment, implementation, experimentation, and adaptation. Structural leaders strive to optimize efficiency and effectiveness in pursuing educational excellence through this methodical approach.

Human Resource Style

The Human Resource leadership style is highly esteemed among educators, resonating with teachers and principals alike due to its emphasis on individual needs and motivations. This approach posits that schools and classrooms function optimally when individuals feel valued and supported within a nurturing and trusting environment. Human Resource leaders cultivate a sense of ownership and commitment among their team members by demonstrating genuine concern for others and actively involving them in decision-making processes.

Incorporating diverse perspectives and fostering collaboration are foundational to the Human Resource leadership style. Many educators find that empowering others to participate in decision-making fosters a culture of ownership and accountability within their school community. Human Resource leaders are recognized as supportive agents of change, leveraging their visibility and accessibility to advocate for the needs of their team members.

This leadership style's heart lies in a commitment to empowerment and advocacy. Human Resource leaders are proactive in providing support, sharing information, and promoting participation at all levels of the organization. Their inclusive approach creates pathways for individuals to contribute meaningfully to the decision-making process, fostering a sense of cohesion and collective purpose. Additionally, Human Resource leaders leverage the organizational trickle-down effect, ensuring that all stakeholders' diverse perspectives and insights inform decisions.

Political Style

The Political leadership style sheds light on the inherent challenges of managing limited resources and navigating complex power dynamics within educational institutions. Individuals and groups often vie for authority in schools and classrooms, leading to a constant interplay of competing interests and agendas. Unlike the rational approach favored by other leadership styles, the Political leader operates in a realm where goals are shaped through negotiation, compromise, and coalition-building.

Conflict is inevitable in this dynamic environment, but it can catalyze growth and innovation when managed effectively. Bolman and Deal (2002) delineate Political leaders as adept advocates who excel at building coalitions and navigating the intricacies of power dynamics. These leaders possess a keen understanding of the organization's distribution of power and interests, enabling them to forge connections with stakeholders and mobilize support for their initiatives.

Persuasion is the primary tool in the Political leader's arsenal, followed by negotiation and coercion as a last resort. By skillfully leveraging relationships and influencing decision-making processes, Political leaders strive to advance their objectives while balancing competing interests. Through their adaptive and strategic approach, they navigate the complexities of the educational landscape, driving meaningful change and fostering a climate of collaboration and shared purpose.

Symbolic Style

The Symbolic leadership style embodies a profound reverence for culture, meaning, belief, and faith within the school community. Just as in any human group, symbols play a pivotal role in nurturing commitment, hope, and loyalty among its members (Bolman & Deal, 2002). These symbols are conduits of shared values, fostering cohesion and guiding behavior through implicit understandings and informal agreements.

At the heart of symbolic leadership lie stories, metaphors, heroes, rituals, ceremonies, and plays—elements that infuse life into the school's endeavors (Bolman & Deal, 2002). Through these symbolic expressions, leaders cultivate an environment where every action carries weight and significance, contributing to a sense of collective purpose and identity.

Drawing inspiration from Bolman and Deal's insights (2003), symbolic leaders view the school not as a mere workplace but a vibrant community where joy and meaning abound. They adopt an inspirational leadership style akin to that of a prophet, casting themselves as directors on the school's stage. In assuming specific roles and orchestrating experiences, symbolic leaders captivate attention and imbue everyday occurrences with profound significance.

Central to the role of symbolic leaders is the discovery and communication of a compelling vision—a beacon that guides the collective journey of the school community (Bolman & Deal, 2002). Through the artful use of symbols, these leaders infuse the school environment with a sense of wonder and possibility, fostering an atmosphere where individuals are inspired to reach their full potential.

In essence, symbolic leadership transcends the boundaries of conventional management, offering a pathway to creating a school culture rich in meaning, purpose, and joy. By harnessing the power of symbols, leaders cultivate a community where each member finds resonance with a shared vision, propelling the school toward collective fulfillment and success.

I have explored various leadership styles within educational settings, drawing on personal experiences and theoretical frameworks. The opportunities afforded by working under different administrators have provided valuable insights into leadership dynamics and their impact on school culture. Through the lens of Bolman and Deal's four-framework approach, leaders are categorized into structural, human resource, political, and symbolic styles, each influencing organizational dynamics in unique ways. The structural style emphasizes productivity and clarity, while the human resource approach prioritizes individual needs and motivations. Political leaders navigate complex power dynamics, while symbolic leaders foster a sense of meaning and purpose through shared values and rituals. By understanding and harnessing these diverse leadership styles, educators can cultivate inclusive and effective learning environments that promote academic growth and holistic development for all students.

Leadership Approaches

Despite significant efforts and resources allocated by national and state authorities to drive educational reform, persistent gaps in student achievement continue to challenge the educational landscape (Ravitch, 2010). Criticisms abound, with some arguing that school leadership appointments are influenced more by political patronage than by the competence of individual principals and the efficacy of their leadership approaches. As Sergiovanni (2001) elucidates, the most impactful leadership approaches positively shape the school culture, fostering an environment conducive to academic success.

Yet, despite recognizing leadership's pivotal role, only a limited number of studies have delved into the leadership styles of urban school district leaders, particularly in Renew and Priority schools, and their impact on student achievement. This study stands out as the sole endeavor to scrutinize principal leadership styles within Renew and Priority schools in a specific urban school district.

Drawing parallels, a report by Useem (2006) examining the school reform efforts in Philadelphia sheds light on pertinent insights. Like the urban school district under scrutiny, Philadelphia underwent state intervention due to dismal student achievement metrics. Consequently, the underperforming schools underwent extensive restructuring efforts. The findings from the Philadelphia study serve as a valuable compass for informing leadership approaches and criteria for principal selection, especially in Renew or Priority schools. Moreover, it offers valuable guidance on enhancing principal training to bolster their effectiveness and clarifies strategic focus areas amidst the pressures of grappling with the label of a failing school.

Echoing these sentiments, Lytel (2013) underscores the importance of inclusive reform efforts prioritizing quality and equity. Central to this ethos is the active involvement of all stakeholders—students, teachers, and parents—in the reform process. Their input enriches the reform agenda and ensures a more comprehensive and equitable approach to driving educational improvement.

The focus is on the critical examination of leadership approaches within the educational landscape, particularly in urban school districts facing persistent challenges in student achievement. Despite considerable efforts to drive educational reform, criticisms persist regarding the influence of political patronage on leadership appointments and the efficacy of leadership approaches. Recognizing the pivotal role of leadership in shaping school culture and fostering academic success, Sergiovanni highlights the importance of impactful leadership approaches. However, limited studies have delved into the leadership styles of urban school district leaders, particularly in Renew and Priority schools, and their impact on student achievement. This study fills this gap by scrutinizing principal leadership styles within a specific urban school district. Drawing insights from a report on school reform efforts in Philadelphia, parallels are drawn to inform leadership approaches and criteria for principal selection, especially in underperforming schools. Additionally, emphasis is placed on enhancing principal training to bolster effectiveness and prioritizing inclusive reform efforts that involve all stakeholders to drive educational improvement with a focus on quality and equity, echoing sentiments expressed by Lytel. Effective leadership approaches are crucial for tackling the challenges encountered by urban school districts and propelling significant educational reform forward.

Theoretical Framework

In exploring the organizational dynamics within an urban district in New Jersey, my study delved into the intricate interplay between leadership styles and school culture, focusing specifically on the distinctions between Priority and Renew schools. Anchored within a robust theoretical framework, this inquiry sought to unravel the nuanced impacts of leadership approaches on organizational dynamics and student outcomes.

Central to the investigation were interviews with administrators, providing rich insights into the decision-making processes inherent within these organizational structures. By juxtaposing the leadership styles prevalent in Priority and Renew schools, I endeavored to uncover the differential effects on staff motivation, decision-making management, and ultimately, student academic achievement.

A critical facet of the study was examining Renew schools—a concept encapsulating institutions that have undergone closure due to underperformance, only to be rejuvenated with fresh leadership and staff. The comparative analysis between the Renew organizational model and the structure of Priority public schools illuminated key disparities. It underscored the significance of leadership styles in shaping the ethos of these educational institutions.

Furthermore, the study delved into leadership styles' short- and long-term ramifications, emphasizing their profound influence on organizational culture and student outcomes. By leveraging data from the report cards published by the NJ Department of Education, I sought to establish empirical linkages between leadership styles and student academic achievement, enriching our understanding of the intricate dynamics within educational settings.

Grounded in theoretical underpinnings, this inquiry sheds light on the contextual nuances of leadership within urban educational contexts. It catalyzes informed decision-making and strategic interventions to foster a conducive environment for academic success. Through a nuanced exploration of leadership styles and their implications, this study offers invaluable insights for educators, administrators, and policymakers poised to drive positive change within educational ecosystems.

In examining the organizational dynamics of an urban district in New Jersey, my study delved deeply into the complex relationship between leadership styles and school culture, with a specific focus on distinguishing between Priority and Renew schools. Anchored within a robust theoretical framework, this inquiry aimed to uncover the subtle impacts of leadership approaches on organizational dynamics and student outcomes. Through interviews with administrators, I gained valuable insights into decision-making processes within these structures, allowing for a comparative analysis of leadership styles between Priority and Renew schools. By scrutinizing the Renew model, which revitalizes underperforming schools with new leadership, alongside the structure of Priority schools, I highlighted significant differences, emphasizing the pivotal role of leadership styles in shaping institutional ethos. Moreover, the study explored the short- and long-term effects of leadership styles on organizational culture and student achievement, leveraging data from the NJ Department of Education to establish empirical connections. Grounded in theory, this research provides nuanced insights into leadership within urban education, informing strategic interventions for fostering environments conducive to academic success.

The Leadership Orientation Survey

The Leadership Orientation Survey, devised by Bolman and Deal (2003), served as the cornerstone of my research methodology, providing a robust framework for discerning the leadership styles of the four principals under examination. Rooted in the acclaimed four-frame model—structural, human resource, political, and symbolic—this survey instrument afforded a comprehensive assessment of leadership orientations, enabling a nuanced exploration of leadership dynamics within the educational context.

Structured into three distinct sections, the survey offered a multifaceted approach to gauge the principals' behavioral patterns, leadership styles, and overall orientation. In the behavior section, principals were tasked with self-ranking their behaviors on a scale of 1 to 5, while the leadership-style section necessitated their evaluation on a scale of 1 to 4, shedding light on their predominant leadership inclinations.

Bolman and Deal's seminal work (2003) provided the conceptual underpinning for the survey, delineating the distinct leadership styles encapsulated within the four-frame model. Within this framework, leaders were categorized based on their responses to the survey, identifying their dominant leadership style as structural, human resource, political, or symbolic. It is imperative to acknowledge that while this categorization offers valuable insights, leadership frameworks can often overlap, allowing for the possibility that leaders may embody traits from multiple frameworks or transition between them based on contextual exigencies.

The essence of my study lay in unraveling the most salient leadership style prevalent among the principals, discerning how their leadership orientations intersected with the specific demands of their roles and responsibilities within the educational landscape. By embracing a nuanced approach that accounted for the dynamic interplay between leadership styles and situational contexts, this inquiry aimed to unravel the complexities inherent within educational leadership, paving the way for informed decision-making and strategic interventions to foster a culture of excellence within academic institutions.

The Leadership Orientation Survey, crafted by Bolman and Deal (2003), formed the bedrock of my research methodology, providing a robust framework for analyzing the leadership styles of the four principals under examination. Rooted in the renowned four-frame model—structural, human resource, political, and symbolic—this survey instrument facilitated a comprehensive assessment of leadership orientations, enabling a nuanced exploration of leadership dynamics within the educational sphere. Structured into three distinct sections, the survey employed a multifaceted approach to gauge the principals' behavioral patterns, leadership styles, and overall orientation. Bolman and Deal's seminal work provided the conceptual foundation for the survey, delineating distinct leadership styles within the four-frame model. Through this framework, leaders were categorized based on their responses, identifying their dominant leadership style as structural, human resource, political, or symbolic. Recognizing the potential for overlap and transition between these frameworks, the study sought to unravel the most salient leadership style among the principals and understand how it intersected with their roles and responsibilities in the educational landscape. Embracing a nuanced approach that considered the dynamic interplay between leadership styles and situational contexts, the inquiry aimed to unravel the complexities of educational leadership, guiding informed decision-making and strategic interventions to foster a culture of excellence within academic institutions.

Competing Theories of Leadership

In educational leadership, many theories have emerged, each offering unique perspectives on the characteristics and dynamics of effective leadership. One prominent theory, Hersey and Blanchard's (1993) situational leadership model, underscores the importance of adaptability, allowing leaders to tailor their approach based on the challenges encountered in diverse situations. This adaptive framework recognizes that effective leadership hinges on the leader's ability to adjust their style to suit the moment's needs flexibly.

In parallel, the Bolman and Deal frames provide a comprehensive lens through which to examine leadership dynamics. According to this framework, leaders typically exhibit a dominant style but possess the agility to transition between different styles as circumstances dictate. The complexity and structure of a given task play a pivotal role in determining the trajectory and duration of change, whether it involves a shift from low to moderate control or from moderate to high control. Additionally, the intellectual prowess of a situational leader significantly influences their adeptness in navigating challenges and effecting change. Notably, visible organizational transformations and improvements under the stewardship of principals often unfold over a span of two to three years, reflecting the nuanced interplay between leadership styles and organizational evolution.

While this research predominantly employs the Bolman and Deal frames as its theoretical underpinning, it is essential to acknowledge other theorists' diverse perspectives. For instance, Hill and Bonan (1991) delve into site-based management, advocating for the decentralization of school decision-making processes. Central to their proposition is granting school leaders and instructional staff greater autonomy, a shift they argue can yield substantial improvements in overall school performance. However, they caution that the realization of such decentralization initiatives has been fraught with challenges, progressing at a sluggish pace. Nonetheless, the autonomy afforded by site-based management can empower schools to craft tailored educational programs, allocate resources judiciously, and enact meaningful changes in organizational and instructional practices. Hill and Bonan's focus on the principal's role within this decentralized landscape underscores the transformative potential of leadership styles in shaping educational outcomes and navigating the complexities of accountability structures.

Understanding Perceptions Using Surveys

Surveys serve as invaluable tools for eliciting insights from individuals, providing them with a platform to express their perspectives and contribute to a deeper understanding of the subject matter. In the context of my research, surveys played a pivotal role in data collection, offering principals an opportunity to share their views through open-ended questions. This approach allowed for a nuanced exploration of individual interventions, enabling a comprehensive understanding of the complex dynamics at play within educational leadership.

The data collection process involved meticulous gathering and analysis of various components to capture the richness and diversity of perspectives among participants. By delving into the intricacies of leadership approaches, the survey facilitated a deeper examination of the underlying factors shaping school culture and organizational dynamics.

Central to this research was utilizing the Bolman and Deal survey, which provided valuable insights into the leadership styles adopted by each principal. This instrument served as a cornerstone in uncovering the multifaceted nature of leadership approaches and their implications for school performance and culture. Additionally, student achievement data from the New Jersey school report card complemented the study's findings, offering quantitative metrics to supplement the qualitative insights gathered through the survey.

Adopting a descriptive case study design, the research briefly summarized the information gleaned from the participants, presenting a cohesive narrative that encapsulated the essence of their experiences and perspectives. Eschewing traditional statistical procedures, the study embraced a qualitative approach, prioritizing depth of understanding over numerical precision. This qualitative lens allowed for a nuanced exploration of the intricacies of leadership dynamics within the educational context, shedding light on the subjective experiences and perceptions of those directly involved in school leadership.

The significance of surveys in the research process is underscored, as they offer principals a platform to express their perspectives on educational leadership through open-ended questions. This method facilitated a nuanced exploration of individual interventions, offering a comprehensive understanding of the multifaceted dynamics within educational leadership. The data collection process was characterized by meticulous gathering and analysis to capture the richness of participants' perspectives, allowing for a deeper examination of the factors influencing school culture and organizational dynamics. Central to the research was the utilization of the Bolman and Deal survey, which offered valuable insights into different leadership styles. Additionally, the supplementation of qualitative insights with student achievement data provided quantitative metrics to complement the study's findings. The research adopted a descriptive case study design, presenting a cohesive narrative of participants' experiences. Embracing a qualitative approach prioritized depth of understanding, enabling a nuanced exploration of leadership dynamics within the educational context. The significance of surveys lies in their ability to illuminate the intricate nuances of educational leadership, thus playing a pivotal role in shaping effective practices within schools.

Transformational Style

Transformational leadership, as delineated by Leithwood and Jantiz (2006), embodies a set of defining characteristics that have been extensively researched and acknowledged in educational settings:

- Charisma: Transformational leaders possess a compelling charisma that inspires and motivates stakeholders to strive towards common goals.
- Capacity Building: They focus on building the capacity of stakeholders, empowering them to contribute meaningfully to the collective vision.
- Collaboration: Transformational leaders foster stakeholder collaboration, creating an environment where diverse perspectives are valued and integrated.
- Motivation: They can motivate stakeholders, instilling a sense of purpose and enthusiasm for achieving shared objectives.

The transformational leadership style resembles the human resource style identified by the Bolman and Deal survey. Leithwood and Sun's (2012) research explored the influence of transformational school leaders on student achievement, revealing small yet significant effects over fourteen years of study. These findings underscored the pivotal role of transformational leadership practices in driving positive educational outcomes.

Howard's (2005) examination of leadership styles categorized research into three main categories:

1. Leadership styles
2. Analysis of leadership styles
3. Applications of leadership styles.

Drawing from Ned Herrmann's brain quadrant research, Howard highlighted leadership as a communication process emphasizing coaching, inspiration, guidance, and support for others. Effective leadership, as posited by the study, hinges on four critical components:

1. Providing direction
2. Generating trust
3. Preferring action and risk-taking
4. Being a communicator of hope.

The literature also identifies four distinct leadership styles, each with its unique characteristics:

- → Type A: Fact-based decision-makers comfortable with logical analysis and data.
- → Type B: Creative problem-solvers who leverage artistic inclinations and flexibility.
- → Type C: Decision-makers are driven by emotions and often ignore facts and research.
- → Type D: Control- and power-oriented leaders seeking dominance over people, tasks, and the environment.

Vroom and Yetton's (1973) study on decision-making processes in leadership classified factors into five groups. These groups are labeled as:

1. Autocratic (A)
2. Consultative (C)
3. Group (G)
4. Group Consensus (GC)
5. Delegated (D)

They highlighted the significance of situational elements in shaping leadership styles and organizational outcomes. Dressler (2001) emphasized the importance of thoughtful decision-making in charter school leadership, stressing the need for leaders to navigate challenges with strategic foresight.

Goldman's (1998) research delves into the profound influence of leadership behaviors within educational settings, emphasizing their impact on staff, students, and faculty members. Influential leaders embody deep-seated values and beliefs, which are evident in their decision-making processes, enthusiasm, and adept management of workloads.

Jordan (1996) provides a comprehensive definition of leadership as the facilitation of others in achieving their goals, emphasizing the importance of technical skills, human relations, and conceptual skills. By exploring various leadership styles and their implications for group dynamics, Jordan's study offers valuable insights into potential strategies applicable across diverse situations.

As research progressed, it became increasingly clear that influential leaders must adopt a holistic approach to leadership, encompassing all four leadership styles. Howard (2005) highlights the dynamic nature of educational leadership, emphasizing how imperative it is to meet regulatory standards while fostering effective communication and adapting to situational leadership demands.

Moreover, transformative shifts in educational leadership, particularly in response to schools facing challenges, are evident. Leithwood (2003) discusses the role of site management, as outlined by Hill and Bonan (1991), and its profound impact on decision-making processes. Transformational leadership, characterized by collaborative relationships and stakeholder involvement, empowers individuals to assume proactive roles, reshaping power dynamics and amplifying the voices of parents, teachers, staff, and students. This leadership approach prioritizes cultivating a collaborative culture, nurturing teacher development, and enhancing group problem-solving capabilities.

The comparative study conducted by Mestinsek (2000) delved into leadership characteristics in charter and traditional schools, shedding light on the evolution of the educational system and its implications for school governance. Specifically, Mestinsek compared leadership qualities and characteristics associated with:

- ★ Transformational
- ★ Transactional
- ★ Laissez-faire leadership styles.

Leaders can use these three characteristics above across educational settings.

In a complementary study, Oshagbemi and Ocholi (2006) explored the diverse spectrum of leadership styles and behaviors exhibited by organizational leaders. Their research ranged from directive to laissez-faire approaches, revealing a nuanced understanding of leadership dynamics. Through cluster analysis, they identified three distinct groups of leaders:

- Practical Leaders: These individuals are characterized by a pragmatic approach to leadership, focusing on tangible outcomes and practical solutions.
- Unity Leaders: These leaders prioritize fostering unity and cohesion within the organization, emphasizing teamwork and collaboration.
- Uncaring Leaders: This group lacks empathy and concern for their subordinates' well-being, displaying behaviors associated with laissez-faire leadership.

These groups demonstrated various dimensions of leadership behavior, including laissez-faire, management by exception (MBE), contingent reward, individualized consideration, intellectual stimulation, inspirational motivation, and idealized influence.

Overall, the research underscores the importance of understanding and applying different leadership styles and behaviors, emphasizing qualities such as:

- Charisma
- Collaboration
- Data-driven decision-making
- Adaptability to meet the diverse needs of stakeholders and organizational contexts.

The exploration of transformational leadership, as demonstrated by Leithwood and Jantiz (2006), sheds light on effective leadership traits in educational contexts. This leadership style inspires stakeholders toward shared goals and fosters an environment conducive to academic success. Parallels with the human resource style from the Bolman and Deal survey underscore the significance of empowering stakeholders and promoting collaboration. Moreover, research by Leithwood and Sun (2012) highlights the enduring impact of transformational school leaders on student achievement. Howard's (2005) examination of leadership styles, coupled with contributions from Vroom, Yetton, Dressler, Goldman, Jordan, and others, deepens our comprehension of leadership dynamics. Comparative studies by Mestinsek and Oshagbemi/Ocholi underscore the need for leaders to adapt diverse styles to meet evolving stakeholder needs, emphasizing the multifaceted nature of effective leadership in fostering positive educational outcomes and excellence within academic institutions.

Notes

Workbook - Chapter Two - Exploring Leadership Styles and Their Impact

This workbook section for Chapter Two emphasizes the crucial role of understanding your leadership style as the foremost action step for educational leaders. It guides you in reflecting on your leadership approach and taking deliberate actions to foster a positive and inclusive environment within your schools. By recognizing how your leadership style influences school culture and the well-being of students, educators, and the wider community, you can personalize and expand upon these exercises to effectively meet the specific needs of your school community.

Understanding and Reflecting on Leadership Styles

- *Question 1:* How does your awareness of your leadership style influence the culture within your school community?

____

____

____

____

- *Reflection:* Think about how your leadership style is perceived by others and how it impacts the school culture.

____

____

____

____

- *Action Step:* Identify your leadership style and list three ways it has positively or negatively influenced your school community. Reflect on how this awareness shapes your interactions and decisions.

____

____

____

____

Fostering a Positive and Inclusive Environment

- *Question 2:* What deliberate actions are you taking to ensure that your leadership style fosters a positive and inclusive environment for all stakeholders?

____

____

____

____

- *Reflection:* Consider the strategies you employ to create an inclusive atmosphere where everyone feels valued.

____

____

____

____

- *Action Step:* Develop a plan that includes three specific actions you are currently taking or plan to take to promote inclusivity. Outline the steps, timelines, and methods for evaluating the effectiveness of these actions.

____

____

____

____

Leadership Style Assessment

- *Reflection:* Complete a self-assessment of your leadership style using a provided leadership style inventory on page 165. Reflect on the results and how they align with your self-perception.

____

____

____

____

- *Action Step:* Based on your assessment results, identify one area for growth. Create a personal development plan with steps to enhance this aspect of your leadership style.

____

____

____

____

Case Study Analysis

- *Reflection:* Read a case study about a school leader who successfully transformed their school culture. Reflect on the leadership style demonstrated and its impact on the school community.

____

____

____

____

- *Action Step:* Write a summary of the case study and compare it to your own leadership experiences. Identify two strategies used in the case study that you can implement in your context.

____

____

____

____

Summary of Chapter Two Insights

- *Reflection:* Summarize your key insights and takeaways from Chapter Two in a paragraph.

____

____

____

____

- *Action Step:* Identify one new strategy related to your leadership style that you will implement based on what you have learned in this chapter. Describe how you will measure its effectiveness.

____

____

____

____

CHAPTER 3

HISTORICAL OVERVIEW

What role do you think school leaders play in comprehending the historical overview of education?

One of my favorite quotes is, "Insanity is doing the same thing and expecting different results," often attributed to Albert Einstein. This quote resonates with me, especially when considering the history of education. When we reflect on how far we've come and the improvements we still need to make in our educational system, particularly for the benefit of children, this quote holds true. How we respond to education mishaps is essential when making improvements. The best way to improve is to understand where we have come from.

The Coleman Report, published in 1966, responded to the underperformance of the education system in the United States. This comprehensive study addressed vital issues, including student performance, school culture, and equitable resource allocation. The report emphasized the importance of parental involvement, school resources, and teacher quality in shaping a child's educational experience. Additionally, it advocated for using standardized assessments to gauge educational opportunities provided by schools.

Following the Coleman Report in 1983, "A Nation at Risk" was released. It evaluated the nation's public schools from kindergarten to twelfth grade. The report highlighted significant deficiencies in the education system and warned of the consequences of growing mediocrity. It sparked widespread concern, prompting political, media, and public attention.

One crucial recommendation from "A Nation at Risk" was the pivotal leadership role principals and superintendents must assume in driving necessary reforms. The report stressed the importance of garnering support from schools and the community. It underscored the need for school boards to provide these leaders with adequate professional development and support to execute their leadership responsibilities effectively.

Between 1990 and 2020, a significant increase in new technologies resulted in the creation of numerous communication tools. This expansion also significantly increased individuals' access to information. The United States experienced a high demand for well-educated workers knowledgeable in mathematics, science, and technology capable of taking independent initiative and working in teams (Ravitch 2000, 430). Consequently, these changes led to a renewed focus on educational reform, prompting the advocacy for school choice. Chubb and Moe (1990) argued that this reform would allow parents to choose their children's schools. Public schools were believed to resist self-improvement due to the influence of various vested interests, such as teachers' unions, school boards, superintendents, and colleges of education. To address this issue, Chubb and Moe proposed a solution that gained popularity and came to be known as the Charter School Movement. These charter schools remained within the school district and were managed by the district. They have since become a significant component of current strategies, and the topic of school culture was explored for school reform (Ravitch 2010).

The GOALS 2000 (Educate America Act) was enacted during the Clinton administration on March 31, 1994. The aim was to enhance student progress and provide schools with assistance to meet academic standards by the year 2000 (Goals 2000, 2011). The reauthorization of the Elementary and Secondary Education Act (ESEA) was explicitly aimed at supporting the achievement of Goals 2000 by offering extra funding for primary and secondary education, improving standards, providing instructional and professional development, and increasing accountability (Improving America's Schools Act 1994, 2011). By 2001, only twenty-two states had adopted standards advocated by Goals 2000. Some states that did adopt Goals 2000 did not offer substantial additional funding or bring about significant changes in their teaching practices. As a result, by 2000, most states still needed to fulfill the mandate set by Goals 2000.

Significant revisions of the No Child Left Behind (NCLB) reauthorization, the Elementary and Secondary Education Act (ESEA), were passed by Congress and signed into law in 2002 by President George W. Bush. This law required extensive reforms in education, and new funding was provided to support achieving these goals. All schools and districts were expected to make adequate yearly progress (AYP) and achieve a 100 percent pass rate by academic year 2013–14. If a school did not meet the AYP for five consecutive years, it was required to undergo restructuring, which could involve reassigning or dismissing all teachers and staff, hiring new employees, or even closing the school.

During the Obama administration, federal mandates were implemented through the Race to the Top (RTT) program, which built upon some elements of the NCLB while introducing new initiatives. For school districts to be eligible for additional funding, unions representing school district employees were required to sign off on the grants. However, this posed a problem for school districts such as California and Maryland, as their unions refused to support the RTT grants due to concerns about potential teacher layoffs.

In addition to various federal initiatives to improve student achievement through funding, states also implemented measures to transform urban schools through takeover legislation. New Jersey, Pennsylvania, Michigan, New York, and Louisiana took significant actions in multiple large city schools by replacing local control with state control and appointing superintendents. Federal funding for education was intended to supplement, not replace, school operations. Consequently, some programs were underfunded or unfunded because states and local communities could not provide the necessary educational resources. Although federal funding came with stringent evaluation rules, it was not until 2001, when the No Child Left Behind

Act became law, that substantial federal funding became tied to student performance evaluations in schools receiving federal funds. According to this law, failure to meet yearly progress goals could eventually lead to school reorganization or loss of federal funding.

In late 2019, the use of educational technology experienced a rapid increase due to the unexpected COVID-19 pandemic that affected the entire world. The NJ Department of Education directed its efforts and support toward digital literacy, ensuring equitable access, enhancing instructional capacity, and planning infrastructure and instructional models that incorporate technology. While there was already a need for technology integration before 2019, this crisis forced the educational system to quickly adapt beyond its previous understanding of technology to serve our youth. The ever-evolving knowledge of technology, school finance, leadership, and school culture remain crucial aspects of school reform.

Reflecting on our educational journey and the ongoing improvements needed, it becomes evident that understanding our past is crucial for making strides forward, especially for the benefit of our children. The Coleman Report of 1966 responded to educational underperformance, emphasizing parental involvement, resource allocation, and teacher quality. Subsequent reports like "A Nation at Risk" in 1983 highlighted deficiencies, urging principal leadership and community support for reforms. The advent of new technologies from 1990 to 2020 spurred educational reform and the rise of the Charter School Movement, aiming for improved access and accountability. Initiatives like GOALS 2000 and the No Child Left Behind Act aimed to enhance standards and accountability, while Race to the Top introduced new federal mandates under the Obama administration. State takeovers of urban schools and the impact of federal funding underscored the complexities of educational reform. The COVID-19 pandemic in 2019 accelerated the integration of educational technology, emphasizing the ongoing need for innovation and adaptation in school reform efforts.

Organizational Reform and Change

For school organizational reform to be successful, leaders must have a clear vision of the changes they expect to see within their school. To achieve significant positive results, it is necessary to understand leadership styles and components of school culture. The main focus of these reforms should be instruction, as it is both a complex and lengthy process. Fullan's work from 2001 emphasizes seven essential lessons that can lead to positive outcomes. These outcomes include:

1. Improved Student Achievement
2. Effective Leadership
3. Enhanced Teacher Professionalism
4. Increased Collaboration
5. Greater Equity
6. Innovative Practices
7. Continuous Improvement.

These positive outcomes reflect the potential benefits of applying Fullan's lessons to educational practice and policy. Improvement should occur system-wide, involving all stakeholders and giving them a voice. Furthermore, it is crucial to approach the process of leading organizational change with care and respect.

Research strongly suggests that the current approach to school reform needs to be revised for our schools, as Ravitch mentioned in 2011. She highlights several essential factors for improving schools, including

- Quality education programs
- Limitations on class sizes
- Investments in teacher development
- The presence of an organized and engaged parent community.

It is worth noting that the 2001 NCLB mandate, which aimed for 100 percent proficiency for all children by 2014, was an unrealistic goal.

In 2015, the National Center for Educational Evaluation and Regional Assistance (NCEE) examined Race to the Top (RTT), a million-dollar funding initiative initiated under the Obama administration. RTT aimed to provide an evaluation framework for underperforming schools. Schools designated as priority schools, receiving funding under RTT, were required to implement interventions such as turnaround, transformation, closure, or restart.

Ravitch (2010) also suggested that educators must go beyond the classroom to fix this broken system. She argued that there is no need for a marketplace to educate our children. DuFour and Marzano (2011) conducted extensive research that revealed how pedagogical skills, effective teaching, high expectations, a warm socioemotional culture in the classroom, engaged students, and an educator who welcomes errors as learning opportunities are all ways to achieve student achievement. Effective leaders who can distribute responsibilities widely are all ways to achieve student achievement.

Successful school organizational reform hinges on visionary leadership, a deep understanding of leadership styles, and the components of school culture. Instructional improvement emerges as the focal point, recognizing its complexity and duration. Fullan's seven essential lessons from 2001 offer a roadmap for achieving positive outcomes, including improved student achievement, effective leadership, and greater equity. However, systemic improvement requires engagement from all stakeholders, emphasizing collaboration and continuous improvement. Ravitch's insights from 2011 underscore the need for quality education programs, smaller class sizes, teacher development, and engaged parent communities. The 2001 NCLB mandate's unrealistic goals highlight the necessity for revised approaches to school reform. Examination of initiatives like Race to the Top reveals the importance of evaluation frameworks for underperforming schools. Going beyond traditional classroom boundaries, as suggested by Ravitch, and embracing effective teaching practices and warm socioemotional cultures, as highlighted by DuFour and Marzano, are crucial for achieving student achievement. Effective leadership, characterized by distributed responsibilities, is key to driving these reforms forward.

School Culture

I have worked with various administrators with different leadership styles, from laissez-faire to dictator. Being overly committed to any style consistently can adversely affect the overall culture. Therefore, leaders must adapt their style according to the situation and switch between styles as needed. Transformational leaders excel in this aspect by effectively understanding the culture and context in which they operate. Leaders must be aware of their dominant leadership style, comprehend the organization's culture, maintain a mindset focused on growth, and implement the gradual release model within the organization. Remember that implementing the following is how leaders can cultivate cultural transformation:

- Know and understand your dominant leadership style
- Have a team that embraces and balances the leadership styles
- Get familiar with the culture of the organization
- Adopt and practice a growth mindset
- Apply the gradual release model to engage the constituents within the organization.

I conducted a comparative study to analyze the leadership approaches of two different types of elementary schools within an urban school district in New Jersey. Utilizing the Bolman and Deal survey (1999), I interviewed four principals from these schools as part of the study's oral history. The interviews evaluated how their leadership approaches impacted school culture and student performance, with questions structured around the 2011 Interstate School Leaders Licensure Consortium (ISLLC) standards (Murphy, Yff, and Shipman, 2000).

My research delved into various aspects of school culture, including staff motivation, professional development, parental involvement, and student achievement. Additionally, I examined student achievement based on established criteria for student proficiency rates in New Jersey, using each school's data to inform my analysis.

The importance of leadership adaptability in shaping school culture emerges as a central theme in the exploration of school culture. Leaders must recognize the need to adjust their leadership styles according to the situation and the organizational context, understanding that a rigid adherence to any one style can negatively impact the overall culture. Transformational leaders, adept at understanding and navigating cultural dynamics, excel in this regard. Key strategies for cultivating cultural transformation include understanding one's dominant leadership style, fostering a team that embraces diverse leadership styles, and adopting a growth mindset. Additionally, leaders should familiarize themselves with the organization's culture and employ the gradual release model to engage stakeholders effectively. Through a comparative study of elementary schools within an urban district, utilizing the Bolman and Deal survey and ISLLC standards, the research delves into various facets of school culture, including staff motivation, professional development, parental involvement, and student achievement. This comprehensive approach sheds light on the intricate relationship between leadership approaches, school culture, and student outcomes, offering valuable insights for educational leaders seeking to foster positive organizational change.

Organizational School Culture

Do you believe school leaders must cultivate the culture of a school to conform with the distinct school community as a means of attaining achievement?

Deal and Peterson (1999) stated that reforms must be tailored to fit the school's unique culture for a school community to thrive. These authors also emphasized the power of school leaders in shaping the culture, highlighting the importance of fostering a cooperative atmosphere and a strong school identity. They also discussed how having a mismatched culture can harm the school community. The school community comprises teachers, students, parents, and the school leader. The authors further identified the essential components of culture as the purposes, traditions, norms, and values that unite and maintain the community, emphasizing the positive impact a healthy culture can have on school reforms. Similarly, research conducted by Sun and Leithwood (2012) discovered that transformational school leadership has modest yet significant effects on student achievement. This study recognized transformational leaders as charismatic individuals who enhance staff capabilities and promote stakeholder collaboration.

Deal and Peterson (1990) analyzed how principals can influence the culture of a school. They examined different leadership styles that ultimately significantly impact the overall culture of a school building. Some styles they identified included the human resource approach, the structural style, and the political style. In addition to exploring similarities in leadership styles, Deal and Peterson (1990) looked at school characteristics, student abilities, and the organization's history. They also discussed the roles of principals, which align with specific leadership styles, and labeled them as symbol, potter, poet, actor, or healer.

Multiple researchers concentrated on enhancing school culture. This book investigates the studies conducted by some previous researchers while also integrating insights from my own experiences. Ediger (1997) noted that as time passed, technology evolved, and students' needs, values, beliefs, and ideologies varied significantly, affecting the school's culture. This necessitated an environmental change. As time went by, opportunities arose for stakeholders to excel and uphold a meticulous planning process. As time continued, the culture and needs of an organization would inevitably change, and it would be crucial for leadership to recognize and adapt to these changes. We witnessed these shifts clearly in 2019 during remote instruction because of COVID-19.

It was suggested that the overall academic culture should change. Ediger (1997) emphasized the significance of establishing a more cohesive culture within academic institutions, where celebrations can occur. This researcher insisted on equalizing this cultural aspect to demonstrate that academics are as important as athletics within the organization. Academics should be regarded as highly as other aspects of school culture. I would definitely argue that every curriculum area, including extracurricular activities, should be respected equally.

As schools work to improve their culture, the faculty, administration, parents, and others must collaborate to ensure that students make the most of their talents. To achieve this, the focus should be on a curriculum encouraging staff to take calculated risks and excel. In 1997, Ediger emphasized the need for staff professional development, support for their efforts, and leadership to create a shared vision and mission with objectives and standards. To improve school culture, there must be a balanced approach between curricular and extracurricular activities, and everyone in the organization must be willing to embrace change.

A 2011 research study by Kullar examined student achievement at four charter schools in California and analyzed how principals' leadership styles impacted school culture. Kullar used Bolman and Deal's leadership framework to evaluate principal leadership and its influence on school culture success. His study aligned with research conducted over the past century, emphasizing leadership's importance in schools nationwide. According to Kullar, leadership plays a crucial role in the success of student achievement and school culture, and principals should take more personal accountability for this.

By referencing the definition of school culture, we can observe the influence of leadership on a school's culture. The environment in which a person works can impact the quality of their job. The role of a principal as a school leader has a significant impact on school culture. To establish a positive school culture, principals must create an atmosphere of optimism. Pepper and Thomas (2002) also presented a detailed summary of a former principal's personal experiences and how she changed her leadership style to contribute positively to her school's culture and boost the confidence of the staff. The principal discussed transformational leadership and how it can create a positive learning environment. She explained how she adjusted her leadership style and the effects of this change.

As mentioned earlier, the scholars' research reveals significant connections between leadership styles and school culture. It's imperative to acknowledge and understand these findings. One key aspect is that leaders often perceive their leadership style differently from how staff members perceive it. This divergence in perception can profoundly impact the school's overall culture. As leaders become more aware of how staff members perceive the organization's operations, they can shape and influence the prevailing school culture.

Furthermore, leaders must recognize that principals' roles have evolved. While they were once primarily responsible for managing day-to-day operations, they now face the additional challenge of balancing managerial duties with leadership responsibilities. This shift is driven by the increasingly complex nature of modern schools.

Bolman and Deal's (1991) research delved into the intricate relationship between leadership dimensions and various aspects of school dynamics, including school culture, teacher effectiveness, and student learning outcomes. Similarly, Edmunds (1982) identified several critical factors associated with effective schools, such as strong leadership, a culture fostering high expectations, an organized environment, and effective communication channels. Notably, Edmunds found that the absence of these factors often correlated with poor student achievement.

In Edmunds's research, parameters included assessing leadership styles, evaluating school culture, and gaining an in-depth understanding of the prevailing school dynamics. These insights are invaluable for educational leaders who foster positive school cultures and drive improved student outcomes.

MacNeil, Prater, and Busch (2009) studied how school culture affects student achievement. Organizational and educational theorists believe that the culture of a school environment is the most crucial factor in student achievement, and school leaders should pay more attention to it. Many instructional, non-instructional, and support staff must fully understand the complexities of leading a school building. According to MacNeil et al. (2009), teachers often need to recognize that their classrooms represent the larger school community and understand how their discipline, instruction, and support within the classroom can affect the overall culture. MacNeil et al. (2009) also emphasized that teachers only become aware of the impact of school culture when they participate in various committees or work on focus groups to evaluate student engagement in the classroom. The authors stressed the importance of school leaders closely examining culture to implement changes effectively.

When we observe the impact of principal leadership behaviors on instructional practice and student engagement, we understand why it is so important to ensure we lead with a meaningful impact. Instructional leadership refers to behaviors that affect classroom instruction (Leithwood 1992, 8). Principals are responsible for being effective instructional leaders and should be committed to informing teachers about new educational strategies, technologies, and tools that promote effective instruction.

Quinn (2002) identified six critical dimensions of instructional leadership:

1. Articulating vision
2. Fostering group goals
3. Providing individualized support
4. Stimulating intellectual growth
5. Setting an appropriate example
6. Having high performance expectations.

According to Andrews and Soder (1987), effective instructional leadership is a crucial factor, and this is evident in schools when the principal excels in four areas: providing resources, being a valuable instructional resource, effective communication, and being visibly present. They also compared instructional leadership behaviors in high- and low-performing schools and observed differences between elementary and secondary school levels. They found a correlation between instructional leadership, student engagement, and instructional practices, confirming the importance of instructional leadership and concluding that school leaders play a significant role in school improvement. This study collected surveys from teachers on the principals' leadership abilities. Also, it involved school-wide observations of student and teacher engagement to provide further insights and confirmation of the findings.

Roach and Kratochwill (2004) conducted a study on evaluations of school culture. They concluded that examining how administrators are perceived within the organization is essential when considering leadership accountability. Assumptions about external and internal environmental factors can also influence school culture. Roach and Kratochwill explained that school culture primarily focuses on abstract concepts rather than individual behaviors. It concerns assumptions, interpretations, and expectations that drive behaviors within the school context.

The researchers employed a mixed-method approach using quantitative and qualitative methods to collect data. Roach and Kratochwill (2004) argued that this combination of methods provides more meaningful results. Their research took a historical approach to evaluate school culture and assumptions and offered practical guidance for measuring these concepts. The authors emphasized the importance of distinguishing between school culture and assumptions and suggested that they should be measured, evaluated, and improved upon separately.

Culture in schools is often likened to the institution's personality. According to Hoy and Sabo (1998), school culture encompasses the prevailing quality of the school environment, influencing the behaviors of both students and staff. Deal and Kennedy (1982) further elaborate, defining school culture as "the way we do things around here," highlighting shared beliefs, rituals, ceremonies, and communication patterns as integral components. They also advocate using various surveys, including the Organizational Culture Description Questionnaire (OCDQ) developed by Halpin (1963), to assess school culture. This tool provides detailed instructions on survey administration and data analysis, facilitating a comprehensive understanding of the prevailing cultural norms within a school.

When evaluating school culture, it is necessary to use a combination of ethnographic methods, such as interviews, surveys, field notes, and participant observation methods, to gather information about school communities and their participants. The research provides background on how to conduct these assessments for each of these types of measurements. Additionally, as part of the evaluation, a study on the quality improvement tools process provides practitioners with tools to examine staff members' attitudes and beliefs regarding work patterns and organizational structure. This study presents a step-by-step approach to assessing school culture.

Teacher leaders play a crucial role in shaping the school culture and how they are supported and empowered to improve it. Culture is developed through social interactions, meaning all staff members involved in the school should be trained and allowed to be informal leaders at some point. Roby (2011) explained that when teachers are not allowed to participate in the decision-making process, it can lead to significant issues related to school culture. The days when principals were the sole decision-makers in schools are long gone. The researcher concluded that teachers who are allowed to contribute to defining and redefining school culture help maintain a positive environment, ultimately increasing student achievement levels. The positive impact of teacher leaders can result in a school culture that prioritizes continuous learning for everyone.

In 2011, Şahin examined the relationship between instructional leadership style and school culture. The study found that an instructional leadership style is essential in defining school culture. It emphasized the significance of building and nurturing positive relationships within the school community. Şahin also discussed various variables that affect school culture, such as feedback, supervision, and identifying and delivering the purpose. The study suggested administrators should be provided with professional development opportunities to enhance their instructional leadership qualities, considering its positive effects on creating positive school cultures.

Throughout the history of education reform, researchers have conducted influential studies focusing on school culture. The study conducted by Wren in 1999 also examined how the hidden curriculum influences the school environment and how behavior affects the practices of school administrators. This researcher analyzed the impact of school culture on the learning environment by studying the influence of teachers and administrators in shaping attitudes and ideas through their interactions. School culture is so deeply embedded in the daily functioning of the school that textbook publishers include reading materials addressing these areas in the curriculum. Wren emphasized the importance of educators being aware of the symbolic aspects of the school environment, such as its culture, as well as considering the perceptions of adolescents and teachers regarding school culture.

Wren (1999) also provided historical context regarding school culture and compared the early years of education (colonial America to the late nineteenth century) with the current cultural outlook of the twenty-first century. In the nineteenth century and earlier, school culture focused mainly on religious and social beliefs and perceptions. During that time, teachers and administrators expected students to conform in terms of behavior and academics, and they closely supervised the school environment. In the twenty-first century, perspectives on school culture have changed, becoming more progressive compared to earlier periods. School culture is now considered the "hidden curriculum" in schools.

Culture is a significant aspect within schools that should not be disregarded, as it plays a vital role in sustaining a prosperous school environment. Schools are paying more attention to their culture, and researchers are trying to provide specific guidelines for educators to assess the implementation of influential school culture. This checklist is divided into four categories:

1. School rules
2. Ceremonies
3. Rituals and routines
4. Document analysis.

It is clear that educators need to be aware of the various aspects of school culture and teacher and student perceptions of it. Wren (1999) believes that understanding school culture will help schools achieve the goal of providing a quality education for all students.

Whitaker (2011) explained the most important aspects of great principals and concluded that the culture and atmosphere of the school are the main factors that differentiate great principals from others. He discussed how perceptions are crucial in school culture and how leaders can turn negatives into positives to promote student achievement and staff productivity. Effective principals guide others in achieving the important goals of their schools. Supporting staff members in becoming effective will help improve the school (DuFour and Marzano, 2009). Effective leaders build relationships so that others are willing to assist them. Self-awareness is a vital skill to develop to make progress. Schools need individuals who are wise enough to offer valuable, constructive feedback. Leaders must be capable of using the feedback productively. Effective leaders know what needs to be done and who to turn to to get the job done. They proactively address potential problems. Effective leaders gather feedback from others and encourage positive ideas from staff and the school community (Marzano 2009; Whitaker 2012).

One way to assess how leaders lead and are evaluated is by establishing the Council of Chief State School Officers (CCSSO) in 1994. This council created the Interstate School Leaders Licensure Consortium (ISLLC) and assigned the organization the responsibility of addressing standards in educational leadership. According to the 2011 standards, six research-based standards are specifically developed to focus on teaching and learning and creating effective learning environments. These standards intentionally cover a wide range of knowledge, attitudes, and performances required for exceptional school leadership. They encompass the diverse knowledge contemporary principals can use as a benchmark for professional excellence. School culture is an essential aspect of the ISLLC and is referenced throughout the standards.

Since the implementation of No Child Left Behind (NCLB) in 2001, states have been required to hold school districts accountable for making sufficient progress yearly (Baker, Betebenner, and Linn 2002; No Child Left Behind Act, Public Law 2001, 107–110). Bredson (2005) and Lazaridou (2007) pointed out that this accountability system uses student assessment results to determine student achievement. Consequently, school leadership has become increasingly responsible for improving school culture and student outcomes (King and Newmann 2001). This shift has resulted in leaders being seen more as instructional leaders rather than just managerial leaders (Bredson 2005; Lazaridou 2007). To improve student outcomes, school leaders need to analyze how their leadership styles affect the educational environment (Martin 2009).

The US Department of Education has tasked the State Educational Agency (SEA) with identifying and providing support and accountability for Priority, Focus, and Reward schools.

In New Jersey, schools are classified into one of three categories based on test scores: Reward, Focus, and Priority schools. Priority schools are underperforming schools with low student achievement rates. The NJDOE state model is to implement the Regional Achievement Center (RAC) process, but one large urban district in New Jersey has implemented an alternative model for Priority schools. RAC support can range from providing additional programs to closing or reclassifying the school.

Reclassified schools can have various classifications, but the focus of my study was to examine the leadership function once schools are reclassified as Renew schools. When a Priority school becomes a Renew school, the district takes several actions. The Renewal process involves replacing 60 percent of the staff and appointing a new administrative team.

Given the assumption that leaders of Renew schools should have higher achievement levels and improved culture compared to Priority school leaders, two crucial questions arise:

1. What are the differences in leadership styles between Renew and Priority schools?
2. How does school culture vary between the two types of schools?

My research focused on utilizing Bolman and Deal's (2003) four leadership frameworks, which include the human resource, structural, political, and symbolic approaches. Additionally, various aspects of school culture were analyzed, such as professional development, staff motivation, parental involvement, and student achievement. Mueller (2015) outlined the three types of schools in New Jersey and discussed how low-performing Priority schools must show ongoing improvement or face potential restructuring or closure.

I conducted informative interviews with four trailblazing principals to discuss their school culture and how they lead. These interviews provided valuable information while allowing these leaders to reflect on the practices influencing their school culture. These leaders offer insight and provide useful examples of situations where they made meaningful changes within their schools. I will provide examples of how they lead and thoughtful accounts of what they would have done differently if given another opportunity.

During the interviews with school leaders, we discussed school culture, and principals shared their perspectives on engaging families and staff. School culture examines how individuals interact and engage within the organization. Parental involvement is a significant component of school culture, and actively involving parents is crucial for fostering a positive culture. School leaders discussed their methods of engaging families and the measures they have in place to facilitate parental involvement. They also addressed their challenges and wanted to create a welcoming and informed family environment. The principals were also asked how they motivate staff and provided specific examples of strategies they employed within their schools to promote staff motivation. Furthermore, principals discussed their approaches to providing professional development opportunities within their schools and shared examples of how they develop their staff.

The examination of organizational school culture underscores the pivotal role of school leaders in shaping and fostering a positive environment conducive to student success. Deal and Peterson (1999) emphasize the need for tailored reforms aligned with the school's unique culture, emphasizing the influence of school leaders in cultivating cooperation and a strong school identity. Their analysis identifies crucial components of culture, including purposes, traditions, norms, and values, underscoring the impact of a healthy culture on school reforms. Similarly, Sun and Leithwood's (2012) research highlights the modest yet significant effects of transformational leadership on student achievement, emphasizing the importance of charismatic leadership and stakeholder collaboration.

Deal and Peterson (1990) delve into different leadership styles' impact on school culture, categorizing principals into roles like symbol, potter, poet, actor, or healer based on their leadership styles. This categorization elucidates how leadership approaches influence school dynamics and culture. Moreover, studies by Ediger (1997) and Kullar (2011) further explore leadership's role in school culture, highlighting the need for adaptable leadership styles and the importance of fostering a cohesive culture aligned with academic goals.

Roby (2011) emphasizes the significance of teacher leaders in shaping school culture, advocating for their empowerment and involvement in decision-making processes. Additionally, Şahin's (2011) study underscores the relationship between instructional leadership style and school culture, emphasizing the importance of positive relationships and professional development opportunities for administrators.

Wren's (1999) historical analysis provides insights into the evolution of school culture, from its early focus on religious and social beliefs to its contemporary understanding as the "hidden curriculum." Furthermore, Whitaker (2011) and Martin (2009) discuss effective leadership qualities, highlighting the importance of creating a positive atmosphere and supporting staff members' growth and development.

The research also emphasizes the need for school leaders to adapt to changing educational landscapes, particularly in the era of accountability ushered in by initiatives like No Child Left Behind. The implementation of evaluation frameworks like the Interstate School Leaders Licensure Consortium (ISLLC) standards reflects this shift, emphasizing instructional leadership's importance in creating effective learning environments.

Overall, the body of research on organizational school culture underscores the intricate relationship between leadership styles, school dynamics, and student outcomes. By understanding and leveraging these insights, educational leaders can cultivate environments that foster student success and promote continuous improvement.

Literature on Parental Involvement

How much do you believe parental involvement plays in the daily functioning of running a school?

Leaders have an important role in encouraging parents to actively participate in the school community through home and classroom connections. School leaders must consider how to establish influences between the school and the community, and more research is necessary in this area (Sanders and Harvey, 2002). The ISLLC also discussed the engagement of the community and the significance of utilizing community resources. Despite the importance of this factor, literature on parental involvement and leadership indicates that only 20 percent of surveyed deans at educational colleges reported that administrators who graduated from their institutions were adequately prepared to involve families (Epstein and Sanders 2006).

Analyzing programs that are intended to enhance schools is essential when examining school culture. In 1982, Edmunds aimed to undermine James Coleman's research, particularly his published report called The Equal Educational Opportunity Survey (also known as The Coleman Report). Published in 1966, this report identified family background as the primary factor determining students' achievements and the fundamental cause of schools being ineffective. Coleman's study concluded that socioeconomic status and family background were responsible for the poor performance of schools, pointing to students from disadvantaged backgrounds as the underlying reason for the lack of success in some schools. He attributed poor school performance to the socioeconomic status of the students. In 1972, Christopher Jencks conducted a follow-up study analyzing The Coleman Report and referencing his findings in the book Inequality: A Reassessment of the Effect of Family and Schooling in America. Jencks's reassessment reached the same conclusions as Coleman's initial study (Jencks, 1972).

The aim was to challenge Coleman's findings by identifying effective schools that successfully educated disadvantaged students. Edmunds (1982) analyzed the methods they employed to achieve this goal. This researcher studied five schools in various parts of America and concluded that some schools effectively educated disadvantaged students, each of which shared five key characteristics. Among these characteristics were instructional leadership and a positive school culture. According to this researcher, these characteristics were interconnected and created an environment conducive to an effective school. He defined each of the five characteristics and referred to them as correlates. His primary assertion was that leadership and culture were the most important of the five correlates, providing evidence that student success did not solely depend on family background or socioeconomic challenges. Instead, changes in the behaviors and individuals within the organization contributed to an effective school. This research presented an alternative perspective to Coleman and Jencks's later research.

The researcher carried out a study on schools that are effective for students who come from economically disadvantaged backgrounds in urban areas. According to Edmunds (1982), urban schools that effectively educate students from low-income backgrounds have strong leadership and create a culture that expects all students to learn. These factors are crucial for a school to be effective. This researcher specifically concentrated on the idea of fairness and explained how to put into practice each of the five factors that contribute to effective schools. He stated that schools must establish an equitable distribution of resources to guarantee that all students can succeed.

This researcher defined equity as a simple sense of fairness in providing necessary resources and services. He emphasized that effective schools, regardless of their location in urban, middle-class, or wealthy areas, should teach all children using the same curriculum and instructional methods. Regardless of their social or economic backgrounds, students should have equal access to the same quality of education as their peers in terms of the following:

- Teaching
- Leadership
- Resources
- Funding.

This approach would promote equity regardless of a child's economic status. Additionally, Edmunds (1982) cited several other studies that supported his conclusions about the five correlates of effective schools. He highlighted the success of urban schools in America while acknowledging the educational disparities. Based on his research, he argued that successful urban schools possessed six similar correlates, including strong leadership and a positive school culture, both of which played crucial roles in their effectiveness.

In my journey through both personal experiences as a parent and professional observations within the educational landscape, I've come to appreciate the profound impact of parental involvement in schools. The creativity required to effectively engage parents cannot be understated. As I've witnessed firsthand, school leaders play a critical role in fostering this involvement, and the level of independence they enjoy significantly influences their ability to cultivate meaningful connections with families.

Charter public school leaders, in particular, have often expressed the freedom they possess to allocate resources towards fostering parental engagement. Their ability to plan and execute parent appreciation celebrations and other activities reflects a flexibility rarely found in traditional public schools where top-down management can sometimes stifle such initiatives. This autonomy empowers principals to tailor their approaches to suit the unique needs of their school community, resulting in commendable achievements and robust family involvement.

As a parent myself, I understand the intrinsic value of parental involvement in shaping a child's educational journey. It's more than just attending meetings or events; it's about actively participating in understanding our children's strengths and challenges, and providing unwavering support at every turn. Having been the first in my immediate family to pursue higher education, I deeply appreciate the emphasis my own parents placed on the transformative power of learning.

I firmly believe that when parents are engaged and involved in their child's schooling, it forges a powerful partnership between home and school, laying the groundwork for enhanced student outcomes. This partnership is rooted in mutual trust, respect, and a shared commitment to nurturing the holistic development of our children. Through collaboration and active participation, parents and educators can create an environment where every child has the opportunity to thrive academically, socially, and emotionally.

In a study conducted by Gawlik (2008), the author examined the degree of autonomy in charter, private, and traditional public schools, among other aspects of school organization. The findings of his study revealed that principals in charter and private schools enjoyed more autonomy than those in public schools.

To measure autonomy, Gawlik (2008) examined the influence of the following on school culture:

- Standards
- Curriculum
- Professional development programs
- Teacher evaluations
- Teacher hiring
- Discipline policies
- School spending
- Parental involvement.

It is important to involve parents in improving schools. Different approaches have been suggested for achieving this, such as through well-structured organizations. Examples of parent involvement can be seen in the existence of Parent-Teacher Associations (PTAs) and Parent-Teacher Organizations (PTOs). In New Jersey's public schools, there are opportunities for parents to get involved by employing parent liaisons who facilitate communication between the home and school. These factors also influence the overall school culture.

The significance of parental involvement in school communities cannot be overstated, with research emphasizing the pivotal role of leaders in fostering active participation among parents. Sanders and Harvey (2002) underscore the need for leaders to establish connections between the school and the community, highlighting the importance of utilizing community resources and enhancing parental engagement.

However, literature suggests a gap in preparing administrators for effectively involving families, as evidenced by the findings that only 20 percent of surveyed educational deans reported adequate preparation in this regard (Epstein and Sanders, 2006).

Historical analyses challenge earlier assertions regarding the impact of family background on student achievement, with Edmunds (1982) presenting alternative perspectives. By identifying effective schools serving economically disadvantaged students, Edmunds argues for the crucial role of leadership and school culture in fostering student success. This research emphasizes the importance of equity in resource distribution and instructional methods to ensure all students, regardless of socioeconomic background, receive a quality education.

Personal observations highlight differences in leadership autonomy between charter, private, and traditional public schools, with Gawlik's (2008) study revealing that principals in charter and private schools enjoy greater autonomy. Moreover, well-structured organizations like parent-teacher associations (PTAs) and parent-teacher organizations (PTOs) offer avenues for parental involvement, influencing the overall school culture.

Facilitating meaningful connections between the school and the community is imperative for involving parents in vital school improvement efforts. By leveraging community resources, promoting parental engagement, and ensuring equitable access to quality education, leaders can cultivate a positive school culture conducive to student success.

Interviewed: Structural Principal Responses on Parental Involvement

"It is necessary for teachers to consistently communicate with parents, regardless of the situation. I believe these conversations are more important to be positive rather than negative, as they prevent parents from feeling attacked when difficult conversations arise. Each child has a communication folder, and teachers are expected to regularly communicate with parents. We strongly encourage them to access online platforms to stay updated on new information and events happening at the school. I have requested a Twitter account to further enhance my communication with parents and keep them informed about what is happening in the school and celebrate teaching activities."

"Parents frequently approach me with various topics. For example, some first-grade parents were concerned about their children learning about Judaism in the classroom. I reassured them that it is indeed part of the curriculum. Similarly, parents have mentioned their second graders learning about the War of 1812. These instances indicate that children are discussing these topics at home, which is perfectly fine. I do not blame parents for not frequently visiting the school."

"I occasionally send out blackboard messages to parents about important information but try not to overwhelm them. If possible, I reach out to them through technology, such as phone calls or flyers, to keep them informed about events and developments. We have a calendar of events displayed near the entrance, so there is always something happening."

"We try to avoid sharing intimidating information, especially when it comes to core knowledge training for parents. Early childhood and elementary grades excel at involving parents in special activities related to literacy themes. We even have a specific day for parents to come into the classroom and participate. Additionally, we hold events with food and other enjoyable aspects to attract parent participation."

"When it comes to eighth grade, I regularly meet with parents since all eighth graders will be transitioning to high school. It serves as a way to ensure their involvement. We recently focused on core knowledge, and students engaged in building pyramids and other hands-on activities. Parents were involved either in the classroom or at home, as evidenced by the projects displayed in the hallway. This indicates significant parental support and engagement."

"We prioritize literacy and provide free books to students, as many other schools do. We have also emphasized the importance of reading for twenty minutes, and a message was sent home to parents regarding this."

"A significant portion of our time is dedicated to assisting students with learning disabilities, including those on the autism spectrum. Many of the challenges we address involve social and emotional aspects."

"We also assist parents in finding job resources within the community. We frequently invite guest speakers to discuss health-related topics. As a healthy new pilot school, we want parents to understand the importance of healthy eating and offer cooking classes. We even have a mini-pantry from which parents can obtain canned goods, accompanied by a recipe on healthy eating. Additionally, we have students with diabetes."

"Parental involvement via face-to-face interactions is not at the desired level. Moreover, it is not ideal to have the same parents involved repeatedly."

"Pre-high school is the grade level that faces difficulties in establishing enough contact with parents. Although contact is made, it is usually focused on addressing struggles rather than celebrating successes."

"We organize events that provide food and other attractions, but these events tend to dilute the intended message. For me, it is crucial to effectively convey the message, whether it is through technology like phone calls or distributing flyers to keep parents informed about school happenings. However, we are not consistently successful in achieving this and it is something that needs improvement. I believe it is essential to designate someone responsible for ensuring effective communication."

"We have a significant number of students with diabetes or who fall on the autism spectrum, which brings several social and emotional challenges to the forefront."

"In the past, when I had more time and fewer responsibilities, I could devote myself to creating newsletters or customized flyers. However, now I lack the workforce to do so."

"It is common to find parents who don't attend core knowledge training sessions or specific programs, and I understand that. This is especially true when dealing with parents who may not have had successful educational experiences themselves."

"Our president of the parent-teacher association (PTA) also serves as a parent liaison to ensure consistency. We aim to prevent conflicting messages by having one person fulfill this role. This individual is already influential at the social level and has chosen to take on a leadership position. As PTA president, they are responsible for answering all parental inquiries and are there to greet parents as they enter the facility. Instead of having a secretary relay messages, parents are encouraged to directly communicate with the PTA president, eliminating unnecessary intermediaries and promoting clearer communication."

"Parent volunteers frequently visit our school. We have a designated parent center equipped with internet access and computers. The parent center is conveniently located to the left of the security desk, allowing parents to access it without needing to sign in. They have free use of six computers complete with printers. Parents can utilize this space for various activities, such as working on résumés or playing games. We intend to create an open and welcoming environment for parents to come and seek support."

"Furthermore, we organize a health fair in collaboration with the community. During this event, the Colgate dental van provides dental services to all students, and we even have a DJ to make it a lively occasion. The health fair is significant; it receives support from numerous community providers, and parents are encouraged to attend."

"We are also in the process of building a new playground in the rear area with the help of non-profit organizations and donations. This playground will serve as a community space and will include features such as a track, turf, areas designated for pre-K, kindergarten, and first grade with game cables, trees, an outdoor classroom, a basketball court, a butterfly garden, and a community vegetable garden. The design of this playground has been developed collectively by the community."

"We also have PTA meetings every month where we provide food. Additionally, on Tuesdays and Thursdays, we run a GED program for parents, and on Wednesdays, we have an ESL program for Spanish-speaking parents who want to learn English. Last evening, as I was passing by the class, the teachers stopped me and said, 'Wait, Ms. ___—they have something to say to you.' They all greeted me. 'Good evening, Ms. ___,' in English, even though they had never spoken English before."

"Furthermore, we organize coat drives every two months, demonstrating our commitment to the community. We are a community school and partner with Union Baptist Church, My Block, My Family, Our Village; Jehovah Jireh; and Rutgers Newark. College student tutors also come to the school during the day to provide assistance."

"Currently, we are conducting a research program with Rutgers Newark and working with GRMC, which will soon have a community van. Twice a week the van will offer medical, dental, and behavioral therapy services for children. Moreover, we are planning to create murals outside and in the back of the school once the playground is completed."

"In terms of community activities, we organize a Thanksgiving dinner for parents, community members, and students on Thanksgiving Day. Additionally, during a holiday celebration, two Santas visit each classroom to ensure that every child receives a toy. Parents also volunteer to help during these events"

"However, we do not allow classroom parties for birthdays. If parents wish to visit a classroom, they should schedule it during the teacher's prep period to ensure instructional time is not disrupted. We only have morning announcements, and no other interruptions occur. Moreover, if a parent wants to drop off cupcakes, it must be done after 2:00 pm. While the teacher can have a party, parents are not allowed to enter the classroom. Birthday parties should take place at home, as our focus is on instruction."

Interviewed: Human Resource Principal Responses on Parental Involvement

"One recent evening I went to court for the fourth time on behalf of a parent. There was another parent who engaged in inappropriate behavior in response to what they perceived as unfair discipline for their child. As a result, the situation escalated and ended up in court. Rather than prolonging the legal process for the parent involved, I opted for mediation as a resolution."

"Granted, I didn't get home until seven thirty that night. The process was lengthy, and it was the fourth time we had been to court. It was a significant matter that I was not willing to dismiss as unimportant. It does matter, and we need to work together. So we ended up collaborating, and it turned out well. As we were leaving we shook hands, and I mentioned that I would be driving back to the southward where I live. I offered her a ride, and she gladly accepted. We even grabbed some fast food, and it was a positive ending."

"During our conversation, one parent asked if there were any job openings at the school, particularly as teachers' assistants. I said I believed she would be an exceptional TA because she understood the needs of children and could advocate for parents and teachers. It's essential to have this genuine collaboration because parents play a significant role in a child's foundational training for the first five years of life. However, we often fail to work together as much as we should."

"I always value parental input, but it's important to recognize that I wouldn't go to a hospital and dictate the programs they should implement for surgeries because that's not my area of expertise. It would be foolish to disregard the knowledge and experience we bring to education. We have different perspectives, and as a result, the majority of decisions should be made by us. However, we can still involve parents by inviting them to sit in, try things out, and gather their feedback on how their children have responded."

"Ultimately, decisions about the curriculum should be made by individuals who have expertise in curriculum development. I believe this is crucial, and though it requires a significant amount of time and effort, it is vital to do it well."

Literature on Staff Motivation

What role do you think school leaders play in motivating their staff?

I am acutely aware of the pivotal role school leaders play in motivating their staff through active engagement. Staff have often shared that providing words of affirmation and being visible are powerful ways to demonstrate how they are valued. It's not just about recognizing their efforts but also about making them feel seen and appreciated for the hard work they put in every day. Staff want to feel valued, and this can also be achieved through collaborative decision-making. When staff have a say in the decisions that affect them and their work environment, it not only empowers them but also fosters a sense of ownership and commitment to the school's mission.

By involving them in the decision-making process, leaders can tap into their expertise and insights, creating a more inclusive and motivating work culture for everyone involved. Previous research on effective schools emphasized the significance of a principal's leadership ability in school performance. Pashiardis (1993) outlined how a principal's leadership style affects school performance and influences the organization's culture. He argued that principals must employ group decision-making to cultivate a positive school culture. Pashiardis discussed several evidence-based decision-making models, including the Vroom and Yetton, Delphi, and nominal group techniques. Each model suggests different approaches to the decision-making process based on the principal's or leader's leadership style. These models advocate for personnel involvement in decision-making and stress the importance of solid decision-making skills in effective schools.

Limited research is available on leadership and school culture in urban elementary schools. School reform advocates strive to provide quality education to all students, which requires transforming school leadership, as noted by Spillane, Hallett, and Diamond (2003). They focused on instructional leadership and highlighted teachers' influence as leaders. Their study suggested that leadership is based on various forms of human capital (skills, knowledge, and expertise), cultural capital, social capital, and economic capital. Meindl (1995) argued that followers are more influenced by their leader's personality traits than his or her overall personality. His study examined followers' ability to follow or form opinions about the leader's leadership style within the organization.

According to Wolf (2007), leaders should prioritize improving learning for all children instead of focusing on minor modifications. He explained that leaders aiming for reform must carefully consider this concept. Those leaders who seek to enhance their organizations must possess vision and knowledge and provide support to teachers, parents, and students to accomplish this task. A leader must have the ability to get the staff on board and involve teachers in the decision-making process. This allows teachers to take ownership and creates motivation for them to adopt new instructional approaches and address students' needs.

This researcher further explains that when a leader has a vision and instills ownership, teachers respond with enthusiasm, imagination, and dedication. A leader's responsibility is to look beyond minor changes and focus on the changes that lead to student achievement. The leader must provide individuals in the organization with tools, resources, support, and guidance to ensure that students achieve at high levels. Wolf (2007) argued that effective leaders encourage participants to improve efficiency by changing practices rather than simply conforming to current expectations.

Engaging staff in collaborative decision-making is crucial for fostering a positive school culture and improving school performance. Previous research underscores the importance of leadership style in shaping school culture and performance, emphasizing the need for principals to employ evidence-based decision-making models that prioritize personnel involvement. Effective leaders prioritize learning for all students and empower staff by instilling a shared vision, fostering ownership, and providing support, resources, and guidance to drive meaningful change and improve student achievement.

Interviewed: Structural Principal Responses on Staff Motivation

"I believe the best time to motivate and inspire staff is at the beginning of the year. Therefore, we will organize group outings and game days to help everyone relax and get to know each other. It is important for staff to feel comfortable making mistakes in front of their peers."

"I try to maintain a professional atmosphere because I want to ensure that people do not feel undervalued. Your paycheck is a way of acknowledging your good work."

"I want to be honest with you and not deceive you. If you are not performing well, I will not tell you that you are doing a great job. I believe in being truthful. I am not the type of person who will compliment you for small things like rubbing a child's shoulders, because that is expected in our profession. Don't expect me to give you coupons or gift cards as rewards, as they are not as effective anymore."

"Unfortunately, my staff has told me they do not hear enough appreciation. This is a challenge for me because I am not aware of everything that happens, and I can't catch every little thing a teacher does. Throughout the day, a teacher may do seventy-five things well, such as wiping a nose tying a shoelace, or even calling parents and thanking them for bringing their children on time, even if they have been late for the past week. I can't notice every single one of these things."

"We make an effort to acknowledge people's birthdays, but we inevitably end up missing someone's birthday from time to time. We also have a sunshine club that aims to celebrate, but it tends to become exclusive, and I'm not a big supporter of it because it takes away from the school's culture. I've noticed more cliques forming this year, which is interesting."

"I believe simply saying thank you and expressing appreciation is important. Occasionally, we include a small special treat, like a piece of chocolate, to let people know that we notice and appreciate them. The most important thing for us is just showing gratitude."

"I'm always on the lookout for workshops or off-site meetings to send you to because I want you to have the opportunity to go out and gain experience. It's still work, but it's a day away from the usual routine. At the end of the day, although it may not sound nice, we are getting paid to do this job."

"Sometimes I may come across something a day or two later, such as Ms. Johnson's accomplishments, and I'll give her a shout-out over the morning PA system or during a convocation. We might bring her up to the front and celebrate her achievements together."

"We have a so-called sunshine club that tries to celebrate."

"We also make a point of recognizing the things teachers are doing well. We give them opportunities to enhance their professional skills and grow, and sometimes we allow them to come in and vent."

"In late August or early September, we usually have game days or fun days where staff can come together and enjoy themselves without any financial burden. We also organize family outing days and other similar events. It's easier to do these activities at the beginning of the year because everyone is not as stressed or overwhelmed."

"I have teachers who arrive at seven o'clock in the morning from Pennsylvania and stay until six in the evening tutoring students. These are the individuals we truly want to appreciate."

"Motivation is easier for me at the beginning of the year, and the holiday season is also relatively easy. We make efforts to do birthday shout-outs. It transforms the culture of the building."

"If a school is designed in a manner that allows teachers to have choices, they can be creative and develop their ideas, and implement their programs. This completely changes the culture of the building. They feel more empowered and are essentially self-motivated."

"One thing I do for the staff is give them the opportunity to make choices. A teacher's assertiveness level may vary between teaching different grade levels. Even if they have certification for a particular grade level, their personality may be more suited for another grade. Teachers are aware of this. So teachers have a say not only in the students they have in their classrooms in terms of behavior and academic level but also in terms of the grade level they teach."

"Instead of adopting a condescending approach, I view my teachers as equals. I see them as my peers. Even though they may not perceive me in the same way, that is how I treat them."

Interviewed: Human Resource Principal Responses on Staff Motivation

"I motivate the staff by creating a culture in which they feel safe and treated fairly, where teachers and staff members feel like they belong to our school community. I have an open-door policy, allowing them to discuss anything with me that is necessary for improving their professional and personal lives."

"In addition, I motivate our staff by leading by example. I want them to come to work prepared every day, so I demonstrate this by always being on time, maintaining a positive attitude, and providing support to our scholars and staff. By being a positive role model, I primarily motivate them."

"I also motivate them by recognizing their efforts. Each week, the administrative team takes turns to show appreciation to the teachers. This could be in the form of small treats, notes on their doors, or something special. This lets them know that we recognize and appreciate their hard work. For example, there is a teacher named Ms. Davis who I pass by when dropping off my kids after a youth group on Friday nights at nine, and she is still at school working. It's incredible to see such dedicated and hard-working teachers, and we want to acknowledge their efforts."

Literature on Professional Development

How much do you think school leaders should be involved in the professional development of their staff?

I acknowledge that the role of school principals in the contemporary educational landscape has evolved significantly, presenting a heightened level of complexity compared to past expectations. Today, school leaders are entrusted with multifaceted responsibilities, assuming roles ranging from caregivers and social workers to policy enforcers and instructional leaders. Leaders play a pivotal role in fostering a collaborative culture among educators, facilitating professional learning communities, and providing invaluable guidance and support to teachers. Pepper (2010) argues that effective principals must balance their leadership styles to promote student achievement.

A more effective way to improve curriculum and instruction to meet student needs is by implementing meaningful and continuous professional development for school staff. This development should incorporate shared decision-making processes in the school (Pepper 2010, 44).

This researcher examined different leadership styles that can impact school performance, including transformational, transactional, and a balance between the two. According to Pepper (2010), principals should combine transformational and transactional leadership styles to encourage faculty and staff to contribute their knowledge and expertise in decision-making processes focused on improving instruction (2010, 49).

The onus of enhancing a school's performance rests on the shoulders of the principal. Depending on the circumstances, diverse strategies may be warranted, compelling principals to assume complete accountability for the academic initiatives and operations of the institution. This can be effectively achieved through a myriad of robust professional development avenues tailored for the staff. Under pressure, principals may adopt a more authoritative leadership approach, where they alone make decisions regarding instructional practices and curriculum development activities within the school (Pepper 2010, 44).

It is crucial that leadership training is prioritized in the reauthorization of the Elementary and Secondary Education Act (ESEA) under the Obama administration. This training should be focused on enhancing the abilities of new and existing principals to balance various skills effectively. Throughout my career, I have had the chance to lead many professional development sessions and have seen the important effect that meaningful professional development can have on educators.

When offering professional development to educators, it is crucial to include, but not restrict, key components, such as

- Instructional technology
- Blended learning
- Social-emotional learning
- Student-centered classrooms
- Gradual-release model.

The evolving role of school principals demands a multifaceted approach, encompassing caregiving, social work, policy enforcement, and instructional leadership. Effective principals balance leadership styles to promote student achievement, as highlighted by Pepper (2010). Implementing continuous professional development, incorporating shared decision-making processes, is key to improving curriculum and instruction to meet student needs. Pepper advocates for a combination of transformational and transactional leadership styles to empower faculty in decision-making processes focused on enhancing instruction. Principals bear the responsibility for school improvement, sometimes necessitating authoritative leadership under pressure. The reauthorization of the Elementary and Secondary Education Act should prioritize leadership training to equip both new and existing principals with the necessary skills. Through firsthand experience leading professional development sessions, I've witnessed the transformative impact of comprehensive professional development on educators, covering vital components like instructional technology, blended learning, social-emotional learning, student-centered classrooms, and the gradual-release model.

Interviewed: Structural Principal Responses on Professional Development

"In my opinion, professional development is crucial and must be consistent. Over the past eighteen months, I have realized the importance of proper planning. Therefore, the first step was hiring individuals who were experts in the program and placing them in the school. This has been the most impactful professional development experience I have been a part of because there has been constant monitoring and evaluation."

"There have been many positive outcomes from this well-executed professional development. It is beneficial for teachers to have evaluative support from someone other than the principal. This kind of support contributes to a healthy and positive professional development environment."

"Before implementing the program, the teachers underwent a two- to three-day training. However, I believe that to evaluate their ability to implement the program, it is necessary to bring in someone who can work alongside them, provide constructive criticism, and offer positive feedback. This level of involvement can't be achieved at the administrative level."

"Teachers greatly appreciate having a voice and the opportunity to fully understand all aspects of the Gold Math program to successfully implement it. As a blended learning pilot school, we have been working with individuals who have been involved in this process with us for the past six months, and there is ongoing support and monitoring."

"That has probably been the most impactful professional development experience that I have been part of. The reason being, there has been consistent monitoring and support. It is personalized by the teacher. Therefore, I believe each teacher requires a unique approach in terms of professional development. We must understand teachers' individual needs and preferences as an educator; whether they are new or experienced, internally or externally motivated, introverted or extroverted, and where they stand in terms of their instructional skills and areas for improvement."

"Hence, every teacher has different requirements. For instance, I had two second-grade teachers who needed the same assistance. After our post-observation conference, we had a discussion where I shared a copy of one of my books aimed at improving teacher practice. I suggested that they read chapter one. Following this, they reviewed the chapter and focused on enhancing their mathematics instruction."

"For each teacher, I try to find a resource that addresses their specific critical needs. I aim to focus on one to two areas for growth, so we can make substantial progress instead of attempting to tackle multiple objectives in a short period."

"Regarding professional development, it varies from person to person. Every individual is unique, and I provide support accordingly. I have a highly effective teacher who performs exceptionally well and is reflective. In this scenario, I advocate for self-reflection before evaluations. We discuss the lesson content beforehand, and after the observation, we engage in discussions about the observations made. Rather than giving direct instructions, I ask for his opinion and use questions to establish a connection. This teacher is already adept at self-support, but I guide him through my thought process, asking similar questions to utilize his reflection for professional development. Therefore, everyone's needs differ when it comes to this aspect."

"For some individuals, it's a conversation; for others, it's a valuable lesson. It depends on where you are on your teaching journey. In certain cases, I will arrange for them to observe another teacher who excels in the specific area they're trying to improve in. This way, they can learn from their peers. Afterward, we discuss what they saw and what they can learn from it."

"Occasionally, they might have a mentor. If there are teachers who possess mentoring skills, we will observe and provide them with feedback. Additionally, if they encounter discipline issues, we have a dean of discipline who can offer assistance."

"I have a new teacher who is facing significant challenges. I have been providing support, along with the dean of discipline and her mentor."

Interviewed: Human Resource Principal Responses on Professional Development

"My perspective on professional development is that we should prioritize both general and individualized professional development. General professional development should address our school's mission and academic programs as a whole. Additionally, we should provide individualized professional development based on each staff member's needs."

"I strongly believe professional development should be delivered directly from experts to learners. I am not in favor of turnkeying professional development because it reduces quality, substance, and effectiveness."

"To sum up, we require general professional development to aid the advancement of our school's programs, as well as individualized professional development tailored to each staff member's effectiveness level. The purpose of our professional development is to enhance the overall climate and culture of our school, particularly in relation to our Leader and Me and Seven Habits programs. Alongside this, we have also received professional development specifically focused on our new math and focus curricula, core knowledge, expeditionary learning, and support programs such as Study Island and similar resources."

"Sometimes, you may be unaware of things you are unaware of. From an external perspective, I can assess your proficiency as a teacher using a framework. If I determine that you are not strong in certain areas, it means you are only partially effective. It then becomes my responsibility to provide professional development (PD) opportunities that will enable you to become effective or highly effective in those areas. We need to work on this together."

"I had a group of three teachers who expressed interest in learning how to use the smart board, but amusingly, they did not even know how to turn it on. They had never done it before and were embarrassed to try it in front of others. So one afternoon, I arranged for substitutes and invited smart board experts to teach them how to turn it on and use it effectively. This is an example of meaningful PD."

"We also had the opportunity to collaborate with ANet, or the Achievement Network, which is dedicated to promoting educational equity for all students. They work closely with our leadership team to help teachers utilize standards and data effectively, aiming for significant improvements in student outcomes. I invited them a couple of times to demonstrate how to use various tools to my teachers. In regard to writing, one of my teachers attended a session and then shared what she learned with the rest of the staff. It was beneficial, as she discussed scoring student writing using standards rather than relying solely on rubrics."

"After participating in A-net and similar activities, I believe my teachers mainly require dedicated time to go through the instructional cycle. They need dedicated blocks of three hours, without the need for external experts to intervene."

"It's just that we can simply sit and say, "OK, let's examine what it is. Now, let's go through the cycle. Let's evaluate this. How are we going to reteach it? And we simply go through that entire data cycle."

So, many times it's just giving teachers the time to do what they know they need to do."

"For a long time, and I don't want to blame our district or anything, I simply think professional development, probably in any field, is difficult. People have the perception that it's a waste of time. I've noticed many teachers taking off those days. I even remember when I was a teacher, thinking that if I had to take a day off from school, I would choose a professional development day over a day with my students because it wasn't valuable."

"Professional development is also very expensive, and I used to save money for it; otherwise, we wouldn't have been able to afford it."

"Teachers don't have enough time."

Interview Insights

The insights I garnered from the interviews with urban educators offer a multifaceted understanding of the intricate dynamics shaping school culture and leadership in educational settings. When I reflect on the research conducted by other researchers, it aligns with my findings. Wren's emphasis on comprehending school culture as foundational to achieving educational excellence underscores the significance of fostering environments conducive to holistic student development.

Whitaker's delineation of the pivotal role of principals in sculpting school culture resonates deeply, highlighting the transformative power of leadership in nurturing thriving learning communities. The elucidation of effective leadership attributes by Whitaker, alongside DuFour and Marzano's advocacy for supporting staff efficacy, underscores the imperative of cultivating leadership capabilities to drive positive change.

The establishment of standards by the Council of Chief State School Officers (CCSSO) through the Interstate School Leaders Licensure Consortium (ISLLC) signifies a pivotal milestone in delineating the benchmarks for exceptional leadership. These standards, steeped in research and reflective of contemporary educational imperatives, underscore the multifaceted responsibilities of school leaders in creating conducive learning environments.

Furthermore, the advent of accountability measures such as No Child Left Behind (NCLB) and subsequent shifts in leadership paradigms underscore the evolving landscape wherein leaders are tasked with not only managerial but also instructional stewardship. The imperative for leaders to analyze their leadership styles vis-à-vis educational outcomes underscores the pivotal role of leadership in driving systemic improvement.

The delineation of school classifications in New Jersey, particularly the transition from Priority to Renew schools, serves as a crucible for examining leadership efficacy and its impact on school culture. By employing Bolman and Deal's leadership frameworks, coupled with a nuanced analysis of school culture dimensions, the research endeavors offer invaluable insights into the leadership landscape of educational institutions.

The informative interviews conducted with trailblazing principals serve as beacons of inspiration, offering tangible examples of leadership in action and reflecting on transformative practices. Their insights into engaging families, motivating staff, and fostering professional development have shed light on thought-provoking areas for improvement, highlighting the multifaceted nature of leadership efforts aimed at cultivating dynamic school cultures.

In essence, the synthesis of research findings and experiential insights underscores the profound interplay between leadership, school culture, and educational outcomes. As educators navigate the complex terrain of educational leadership, these insights serve as guiding lights, illuminating pathways toward fostering inclusive, equitable, and thriving learning environments for all students.

Notes

Workbook - Chapter Three - Historical Overview

This workbook section for Chapter Three is crafted to assist educational leaders in introspecting on their roles and actions concerning understanding historical contexts, cultivating school culture, involving parents, motivating staff, and supporting professional development. It encourages practical steps to amplify their leadership impact and foster a positive educational environment.

Understanding the Historical Context of Education

- *Question 1:* What role do you think school leaders play in comprehending the historical overview of education?

____

____

____

____

- *Reflection:* Reflect on the importance of understanding the history of education in your leadership role.

____

____

____

____

- *Action Step:* Research and write a summary of a significant historical event in education. Discuss how this event has influenced current educational practices and how it informs your leadership approach.

Cultivating School Culture

- *Question 2:* Do you believe school leaders must cultivate the culture of a school to conform with the distinct school community as a means of attaining achievement?

- *Reflection:* Consider the relationship between school culture and the unique characteristics of the school community.

- *Action Step:* Outline three specific strategies you use or plan to use to align your school's culture with its community. Include steps to implement these strategies and ways to measure their success.

Parental Involvement in Schools

- *Question 3:* How much do you believe parental involvement plays in the daily functioning of running a school?

- *Reflection:* Reflect on the role of parents in the school community and their impact on school operations.

- *Action Step:* List two examples of effective parental involvement initiatives you have implemented or observed. Describe the outcomes and how these initiatives contributed to the school's success.

____

____

____

____

Motivating Staff

- *Question 4:* What role do you think school leaders play in motivating their staff?

____

____

____

____

- *Reflection:* Think about how your leadership can inspire and motivate your staff.

____

____

____

____

- *Action Step:* Identify three motivational strategies you use or plan to use to boost staff morale. Detail how you will implement these strategies and track their effectiveness.

____

____

____

____

Involvement in Professional Development

- *Question 5:* How much do you think school leaders should be involved in the professional development of their staff?

____

____

____

____

- *Reflection:* Reflect on the importance of professional development and your role in facilitating it.

____

____

____

____

- *Action Step:* Develop a professional development plan for your staff. Include specific training sessions, workshops, or other opportunities, and describe how you will support and encourage staff participation.

Outline methods for evaluating the impact of these professional development activities.

____

____

____

____

Summary of Chapter Three Insights

- *Reflection:* Summarize your key insights and takeaways from Chapter Three in a concise paragraph.

____

____

____

____

- *Action Step:* Identify one new strategy related to the historical overview, school culture, parental involvement, staff motivation, or professional development that you will implement based on what you have learned in this chapter. Describe how you will measure its effectiveness and the impact it aims to achieve.

____

____

____

____

CHAPTER 4

THE EVOLUTION OF LEADERSHIP STYLE

To what extent do you believe the leadership styles implemented in your district have influenced the cultivation of either a positive or negative school culture?

Understanding leadership styles and their impact on school culture is crucial for the progress and success of any school district. Elmore (2003) pointed out the necessity for principals to receive adequate preparation for their roles, especially considering the demands imposed by initiatives like No Child Left Behind (NCLB). The mandates set by federal and state authorities aimed at improving test scores often create pressure for administrators to adopt authoritarian approaches, leading to unilateral decision-making regarding instructional practices.

Implementing a top-down leadership style often manifests in reactive measures such as establishing Saturday academies and before- and after-school tutoring sessions. While these interventions may bolster academic performance and meet mandated testing goals, they inadvertently underscore a concerning trend: prioritizing test-related content over holistic educational approaches.

Reliance on repetitive test preparation methods risks narrowing the educational experience, potentially neglecting students' diverse learning needs and interests. Focusing predominantly on standardized testing outcomes risks overlooking crucial aspects of education such as critical thinking, creativity, and social-emotional development. This narrow focus may inadvertently stifle innovation and curiosity, hindering the cultivation of well-rounded, engaged learners.

Moreover, the pressure to perform well on standardized tests can create an atmosphere of stress and anxiety among students, detracting from their overall well-being and negatively impacting their motivation to learn. This myopic emphasis on test scores can undermine the broader goal of education, which encompasses the cultivation of lifelong learners equipped with the skills and knowledge necessary for success in an ever-changing world.

It is imperative to critically evaluate the efficacy of such interventions and consider alternative approaches that prioritize a more comprehensive and student-centered educational experience. By embracing a holistic approach to education that values diverse learning opportunities and fosters a culture of inquiry and exploration, schools can better meet the multifaceted needs of their students and cultivate a vibrant and enriching learning environment.

Fostering Inclusivity in School Decision-Making

Pashiards (1993) underscored the pivotal role of shared decision-making in fostering a dynamic and inclusive school environment. Embracing a collaborative approach to decision-making empowers stakeholders and cultivates a sense of ownership and investment in the school community's collective vision and mission.

When staff members and parents are actively involved in the decision-making process, they feel valued and respected, increasing morale, job satisfaction, and commitment. School leaders can tap into the community's wealth of knowledge and expertise by soliciting input from diverse perspectives, leading to more informed and effective decisions.

Shared decision-making promotes transparency and accountability, as decisions are made collaboratively and with the collective interest of the school community in mind. This fosters trust and cohesion, strengthening stakeholder relationships and enhancing the school culture. Involving staff and parents in decision-making can lead to innovative solutions and creative problem-solving approaches. By leveraging the community's collective wisdom and creativity, schools can adapt more swiftly to challenges and seize opportunities for growth and improvement.

Ultimately, a culture of shared decision-making not only motivates stakeholders but also fosters a sense of belonging and shared responsibility for the success and well-being of all members of the school community. By embracing collaboration and inclusivity, schools can cultivate a vibrant and resilient learning environment where everyone feels valued, empowered, and inspired to contribute towards common goals.

School leaders must enhance their abilities to manage different leadership styles effectively and recognize the correlation between leadership approaches and school culture. By promoting shared decision-making and prioritizing strategies that motivate and engage the entire school community, leaders can create a positive school culture conducive to academic success and holistic student development.

Transformational and transactional leadership styles are crucial for success in a high-stakes environment. According to Pepper (2010, 8), by combining transformational and transactional leadership styles, principals enable faculty and staff to contribute their knowledge and expertise in decision-making focused on improving instruction and curriculum aligned with a shared vision. Interestingly, a school's success is measured by the effectiveness of its leaders. The accountability of school leaders is tied to the quality of instruction delivered by teachers and the learning outcomes of students (Dinham 2005; Fullan 2002; Sergiovanni 2001). This is necessary to ensure high-quality instruction (Hallinger 2003; Hickey and Harris 2005; Leithwood and Riehl 2003; and Stewart 2006).

Ensuring high-quality instruction necessitates robust professional development for teachers. Pepper and Thomas (2002) underscored the symbiotic relationship between school culture and leadership. Utilizing the Bolman and Deal frames for evaluating leadership styles (Deal and Peterson, 1990) is imperative to grasp their influence on school culture.

Typically, school leaders are evaluated by superintendents. However, in my experience as a vice/principal, integrating anonymous feedback evaluations from staff members proved transformative for leadership effectiveness. This approach not only cultivates a culture of continuous improvement but also ensures alignment with the evolving needs of the school community. Superintendents should engage more with individual schools to fully understand their dynamics. Implementing this practice yielded significant positive outcomes during my tenure, notably when staff witnessed their feedback incorporated into my daily leadership practices.

Understanding leadership styles and their influence on school culture is the cornerstone of fostering progress and ensuring the success of every school district. Elmore (2003) highlights the necessity for principals to receive adequate preparation, especially in light of initiatives like No Child Left Behind (NCLB). However, the pressure to improve test scores often results in adopting top-down leadership styles, focusing on test-related content and unilateral decision-making, potentially neglecting students' diverse learning needs.

Pashiards (1993) stresses the importance of shared decision-making to foster inclusivity, empowerment, and transparency within the school environment. Involving staff and parents in decision-making processes enables schools to tap into diverse perspectives, enhance morale, and drive innovation.

Pepper (2010) advocates for a blend of transformational and transactional leadership styles to engage faculty and staff in decision-making to improve instruction. Effective school leaders must manage different leadership styles to create a positive environment conducive to academic success and holistic student development.

Integrating anonymous feedback evaluations from staff members, as observed in the author's experience, can significantly enhance leadership effectiveness and promote a culture of continuous improvement. Superintendents are encouraged to engage more with individual schools to understand their dynamics better and align with evolving needs, fostering positive outcomes.

School Leaders As Change Agents

Drawing from personal experience and existing research, it is evident that principals serve as linchpins in driving transformative change within school communities. They wield considerable influence in shaping their schools' culture, climate, and educational outcomes. Amidst the wealth of research on educational leadership and the pivotal role of principals, a conspicuous void persists in literature - one that delves specifically into urban school leadership styles and their profound impact on school culture.

Urban schools often face unique challenges from socioeconomic disparities, cultural diversity, and resource constraints. Consequently, the leadership approaches employed in these contexts can have profound implications for student achievement, teacher morale, and community engagement. Despite the dearth of targeted research in this area, understanding urban school leadership styles must be addressed in addressing the complex needs of diverse student populations.

From my observations and interactions within urban school settings, it is clear that effective leadership is paramount in navigating the intricate dynamics of urban education. Principals must possess strong instructional leadership skills and a deep understanding of the socio-cultural context in which their schools operate. They must be adept at fostering collaboration, cultivating trust, and promoting equity to create inclusive and supportive learning environments for all students.

Research suggests that principals' leadership styles significantly influence school culture, teacher retention rates, and student outcomes. However, the nuanced interplay between leadership styles and urban school contexts necessitates further exploration to inform evidence-based practices and policy interventions tailored to these settings. While the literature on urban school leadership may be limited, understanding and addressing the unique challenges facing urban schools remains urgent. By bridging the gap between research and practice, educators, policymakers, and school leaders can collaborate to develop innovative solutions that empower urban schools to provide high-quality education and equitable opportunities for all students.

Numerous studies have underscored the profound influence of effective leadership styles wielded by principals on school culture. Barr (2006) and Shaw (2009) have documented the positive correlation between principal leadership styles, teacher motivation, and student achievement, highlighting the critical role principals play in shaping the overall ethos of their schools.

While acknowledging the scarcity of research in this domain, we must prioritize the exploration of leadership styles and their ramifications on school culture in urban settings. Peterson and Deal (1998) emphasized the importance of principals understanding their schools' historical contexts and purposes, underscoring the need for effective leadership to foster accountability within school cultures.

Kelly, Thornton, and Daugherty (2005) echoed the necessity for effective principals in creating learning environments conducive to accountability. Blanchard and Johnson (2001) stressed that leaders must exert control in steering school cultures toward predefined goals.

My study, conducted in an urban New Jersey school, examined the dominant leadership styles of principals in Renew and Priority schools using the Bolman and Deal (2003) four-frame model and revealed intriguing insights. Both Priority school principals exhibited a dominant human resources leadership style, aligning with their interview responses. Conversely, Renew school principals showcased a predominant structural leadership style, albeit with nuances of the human resources frame evident in their interviews, as identified through the Bolman and Deal survey.

This study unequivocally underscores the pivotal role of effective leadership in molding school culture and the imperative for further investigation within urban educational contexts. Sullivan and Glanz (2006) aptly recognized that reforming school leadership practices enhances student performance and cultivates a thriving school culture. Central to this endeavor is the unwavering commitment of principals and staff in setting and pursuing student improvement goals.

Similarly, the insights of Ubben, Hughes, and Norris (2015) resonate, emphasizing the paramount importance of principals in fostering a supportive environment among teachers and the community to realize the school's objectives. Consequently, principals who possess a deep understanding of their leadership styles and adeptly leverage them to foster positive school culture through parental involvement, maintaining staff morale, managing student discipline, and providing professional development opportunities are poised to elevate student success significantly.

School leaders serve as change agents, driving transformation through their leadership styles, strategic vision, and commitment to fostering a positive school culture conducive to student achievement and growth. Further exploration and understanding of these dynamics in urban educational contexts are essential for effective leadership and sustainable improvement.

Drawing from personal experiences and existing research, school leaders are recognized as pivotal change agents in driving transformative change within school communities. Their profound influence extends to shaping school culture, climate, and educational outcomes, particularly in the complex context of urban schools. While the literature on urban school leadership is limited, there is an urgent need to comprehend and tackle the distinctive challenges encountered in these environments. Effective leadership, characterized by strong instructional leadership skills and a deep understanding of socio-cultural contexts, is essential for creating inclusive and supportive learning environments.

The research underscores the significant impact of principal leadership styles on school culture, teacher retention rates, and student outcomes, highlighting the need for further exploration and evidence-based practices tailored to urban settings. By prioritizing the exploration of leadership styles and their implications on school culture, educators, policymakers, and school leaders can collaborate to develop innovative solutions that empower urban schools to provide high-quality education and equitable opportunities for all students.

Action Plan for Great Leaders

How do you assess the correlation between leadership styles and the morale, engagement, and performance of staff and students within your schools? In what ways do you think the leadership styles exhibited by school administrators impact the level of trust and collaboration among teachers, students, and parents?

I strongly believe that the action plan for great leaders is deeply rooted in a holistic approach that prioritizes continuous learning, introspection, and an unwavering commitment to cultivating an environment conducive to the flourishing of all stakeholders.

Recognizing the pivotal role of leadership in shaping school culture and student outcomes, I firmly advocate for leaders to immerse themselves in continuous professional development, honing their skills and strategies. This unwavering commitment to personal and professional growth is imperative for instigating positive transformations within educational settings.

Goleman's seminal research 2000 emphasized the correlation between different leadership styles and various facets of emotional intelligence. Leaders with high emotional intelligence adeptly navigate the intricacies of interpersonal relationships, fostering trust and collaboration within their teams. Moreover, studies by Deal and Peterson (1990) and Marzano, Waters, and McNulty (2005) shed light on the intricate relationships between leadership styles, school culture, and student achievement, underscoring the critical importance of effective leadership in shaping the educational landscape.

At the heart of this action plan lies a profound understanding of the intricate dynamics of leadership styles and emotional intelligence. Leaders must demonstrate proficiency in various leadership approaches and possess the emotional acuity to navigate complex interpersonal relationships and drive meaningful change.

To achieve this, leaders should actively participate in continuous professional development, seizing opportunities to expand their knowledge base, refine leadership techniques, and stay abreast of emerging trends and best practices in education. This may entail attending workshops, conferences, and seminars and pursuing advanced degrees or certifications in educational leadership.

Self-reflection is crucial in a leader's journey toward excellence. By regularly evaluating their strengths, areas for growth, and the impact of their leadership style on the school community, leaders can gain valuable insights and identify areas for improvement. Feedback from peers, mentors, and staff members is valuable for enhancing leadership effectiveness.

In addition to personal development, great leaders prioritize fostering a positive and inclusive school culture characterized by collaboration, trust and shared vision. This involves creating platforms for meaningful dialogue and collaboration among staff, students, parents, and community members, empowering all stakeholders to contribute to the school's goals and aspirations.

Great leaders recognize the significance of modeling behavior that aligns with the school community's values and expectations. By exemplifying integrity, empathy, and a commitment to equity and diversity, leaders inspire trust and confidence among their team members and cultivate a mutual respect and support culture.

The action plan for great leaders is an ongoing and adaptive process that evolves in response to the changing needs and circumstances of the school community. By embracing a mindset of continuous improvement and dedicating themselves to serving the needs of all stakeholders, great leaders can drive positive change, foster innovation, and create an environment where every individual has the opportunity to thrive and succeed.

As we embark on crafting the action plan for exceptional leaders, it becomes evident that its impact extends far beyond the realm of education to shape the future of society itself. Grounded in a comprehensive ethos that values ongoing learning, emotional intelligence, and the steadfast nurturing of inclusive environments, this action plan stands as a beacon of transformation for educational leaders.

Drawing from the groundbreaking research of Goleman and the profound insights offered by scholars such as Deal, Peterson, Marzano, Waters, and McNulty, we uncover the intricate dynamics linking leadership styles, school culture, and student achievement. Armed with this wealth of knowledge, leaders are empowered to deftly navigate the complexities of interpersonal relationships and enact meaningful change within their schools.

The journey of leadership is one of ongoing development and self-reflection. Leaders must actively engage in continuous professional development, embrace feedback, and model behaviors aligned with the values of their school community. By fostering a positive and inclusive culture characterized by collaboration and shared vision, great leaders empower all stakeholders to contribute to the school's collective goals and aspirations.

As we look to the future, we recognize that the action plan for great leaders is not static but adaptive, evolving in response to the changing needs and circumstances of the school community. By embracing a mindset of continuous improvement and dedicating themselves to serving the needs of all stakeholders, great leaders have the power to drive positive change, foster innovation, and create environments where every individual can thrive and succeed.

Let us carry forth the lessons learned from this action plan with courage and conviction, knowing that our leadership has the potential to shape the landscape of education and society for generations to come. Together, we embark on a journey of transformation guided by the principles of continuous learning, emotional intelligence, and unwavering commitment to the flourishing of all.

Before we delve into educational practices, let's recap the foundational elements of our action plan:

1. Holistic Leadership Approach:Prioritize continuous learning and create conducive environments for stakeholder flourishing.
2. Continuous Development:Advocate for ongoing personal and professional growth to positively shape school culture and student outcomes.
3. Understanding Leadership Dynamics: Utilize emotional intelligence and leadership research to navigate relationships effectively and drive meaningful change.

4. Foster Positive Culture: Cultivate dialogue, collaboration, and integrity to inspire trust and mutual respect within the school community.
5. Adaptive Leadership: Recognize leadership as an ongoing, adaptive process, guided by continuous improvement and dedication to stakeholder needs.

Educational Practices

Step into the vibrant landscape of educational practices, where the odyssey towards profound transformative leadership unfolds. As we delve into the intricate variations of educational transformation, we are confronted with the imperative need for a proactive strategy that seamlessly integrates observation with data-driven insights. At its core, this strategy ignites profound cultural metamorphosis within our schools.

Embarking on a journey of discovery, we seek to uncover the core of educational leadership that cultivates openness, collaboration, and inclusivity among educators. It is imperative to delve into the pivotal role of school principals as advocates of these principles, establishing the foundation for transparent and supportive school cultures.

Our exploration takes us through the vital mechanisms that drive continuous improvement, from monthly principals' meetings that refine leadership practices to comprehensive end-of-year surveys that perpetually assess school culture and leadership effectiveness. Through transparent dissemination of survey results and thoughtful discussions, we will witness the transformative power of data-driven decision-making in propelling educators and students toward greater success.

Leveraging my wealth of experience and deep insights, I champion collaborative partnerships between district-level administrators and local higher education institutions. I underscore the indispensable value of mentorship programs and tailored professional development initiatives in cultivating the next generation of leaders.

Now, let's explore the significance of tailored support for school culture, particularly in urban districts. Here, strong administrative leadership and precisely targeted initiatives are paramount for effectively tackling distinct objectives.

As we navigate the complexities of educational practices, we will uncover the transformative power of understanding key leadership factors and embracing a holistic approach to educational leadership. Through dedication, innovation, and a commitment to lifelong learning, we will embark on a journey to create school cultures where curiosity thrives, diversity is celebrated, and everyone feels valued and supported.

Embark on this profound transformative journey, where the impact of transformative leadership knows no bounds, leaving an indelible legacy of inspiration and growth for future generations. In this endeavor, you mold the future of education and society—becoming a visionary change-maker.

Implementing a proactive strategy that seamlessly blends observation with data-driven insights is not just beneficial—it's essential. This strategy serves as the cornerstone for igniting a profound cultural transformation within schools. By actively observing and collecting data on various aspects of school culture, teaching methodologies, and student performance, educators can gain invaluable insights into the strengths and weaknesses of current practices.

The true power of this proactive strategy lies in identifying principals whose leadership styles are uniquely suited to fostering an atmosphere of openness and collaboration among educators. These visionary leaders possess the ability to inspire and empower their teams, creating a culture where ideas are freely exchanged, feedback is welcomed, and collective goals are pursued with enthusiasm.

Through their leadership, principals can cultivate an environment where teachers feel valued and supported, encouraging them to experiment with new teaching methods, collaborate on interdisciplinary projects, and engage in ongoing professional development. This collaborative spirit enhances the overall quality of education and fosters a sense of belonging and camaraderie among staff members.

Furthermore, when supported by data-driven insights, these leaders can make informed decisions that have a tangible impact on student learning outcomes. By analyzing student performance data, identifying areas for improvement, and implementing targeted interventions, principals can ensure that every student receives the support they need to succeed academically.

In essence, the proactive integration of observation with data-driven insights empowers principals to lead their schools through continuous improvement and innovation. By fostering a culture of openness and collaboration, these leaders can inspire positive change and create an environment where educators and students thrive.

Empowering school principals to champion educational principles and ensuring their sustained implementation district-wide is pivotal to fostering an inclusive and transparent school culture. These principles encompass academic excellence and values such as equity, diversity, and community engagement. By entrusting principals with the responsibility to advocate for and uphold these principles, schools can create an environment where every student feels valued, supported, and motivated to succeed.

Monthly principals' meetings serve as a cornerstone in this endeavor, providing a dedicated platform for leaders to collaborate and enhance educational practices. During these meetings, principals can share insights, experiences, and challenges, drawing upon a wealth of local, state, and national resources. From research findings to innovative strategies, these meetings facilitate the exchange of best practices and encourage continuous learning among educational leaders.

These meetings are not just about discussing leadership practices but also about refining behaviors and fostering a culture of accountability and reflection. Principals engage in candid discussions about their leadership approaches, seeking feedback from colleagues and identifying areas for growth. Through this collaborative process, principals can refine their leadership skills, deepen their understanding of effective educational practices, and ultimately, better serve their schools and communities.

Additionally, active engagement in professional organizations further enriches principals' knowledge and skills, providing access to cutting-edge research, networking opportunities, and ongoing professional development. By participating in conferences, workshops, and seminars, principals stay abreast of the latest trends and innovations in education, enabling them to make informed decisions and lead confidently.

As we navigate through these educational practices, we witness the transformative power of understanding key leadership factors and embracing continuous learning. Let's dive into the critical components of these practices, emphasizing their significance in driving positive change and fostering excellence within educational environments.

- → Proactive Strategy Integration: Seamlessly blend observation with data-driven insights to ignite profound cultural transformation within schools.
- → Identifying Visionary Leaders:Recognize principals who foster openness and collaboration among educators, inspiring and empowering their teams to pursue collective goals with enthusiasm.
- → Cultivating Collaborative Environments: Create a culture where ideas are freely exchanged, feedback is welcomed, and ongoing professional development is encouraged among educators.
- → Informed Decision-Making: Utilize data-driven insights to inform decisions that tangibly impact student learning outcomes, ensuring every student receives the support they need to succeed.
- → Monthly Principals' Meetings: Provide dedicated platforms for collaborative learning, resource sharing, and continuous improvement, fostering a culture of accountability and reflection among educational leaders.

Harnessing Surveys for Transformative Educational Practices

In our quest to advance educational practices, empowering school principals and fostering a culture of collaboration and continuous improvement stand as essential pillars. Yet, to truly catalyze transformation in practice, we must embrace the strategic incorporation of surveys. These surveys serve as vital instruments, enabling us to gather diverse perspectives and insights from stakeholders, thereby informing decision-making, fostering transparency, and driving collective progress.

Comprehensive end-of-year surveys conducted by school districts play a crucial role in continually assessing school culture and evaluating the effectiveness of principals' leadership styles. These surveys serve as invaluable tools for gaining insights into the perceptions and experiences of various stakeholders within the school community.

Administered to leaders, teachers, students, and parents, these surveys aim to capture a diverse range of perspectives on the prevailing school culture and the impact of principals' leadership approaches. By soliciting feedback from all members of the school community, these surveys provide a comprehensive picture of the educational environment's strengths, weaknesses, and areas for improvement.

The insights gleaned from these surveys are instrumental in informing efforts to enhance school culture and drive positive change. School leaders can develop targeted strategies to address issues and build upon successes by identifying areas of alignment and discrepancies between different stakeholders' perceptions. For example, initiatives can be implemented to improve transparency and collaboration if the surveys reveal a need for more communication between the administration and teachers. Similarly, if students or parents express concerns about safety or inclusivity, interventions can be implemented to create a more supportive and welcoming environment.

Additionally, the data gathered from these surveys can predict student achievement. By analyzing correlations between survey responses and academic outcomes, school leaders can identify factors contributing to student success and prioritize interventions accordingly. For instance, if survey data indicates high student engagement and satisfaction with teaching methods, educators can leverage these strategies to enhance learning outcomes across the board.

Overall, comprehensive end-of-year surveys are indispensable tools for assessing school culture, evaluating leadership effectiveness, and driving continuous improvement in educational practices. By leveraging the insights gleaned from these surveys, schools can cultivate a positive and supportive learning environment that fosters all students' academic success and holistic development.

Transparent dissemination of survey results and engaging in thoughtful discussions regarding their implications are essential components of the evaluative process within educational practices. School districts promote accountability, transparency, and a sense of ownership in the improvement process by openly sharing survey findings with all stakeholders, including administrators, teachers, students, and parents.

When survey results are readily available to the entire school community, it fosters a culture of openness and trust. It allows stakeholders to understand the strengths and weaknesses identified through the surveys, encouraging collective reflection and problem-solving. This transparency also ensures that all school community members have a clear understanding of the current state of affairs, empowering them to contribute to meaningful change.

I have observed the profound impact of engaging in deliberate and insightful discussions about the implications of survey results on driving continuous improvement. These discussions allow stakeholders to delve deeper into the data, analyze trends, and identify areas for growth. By facilitating constructive dialogue, school districts can harness the community's collective wisdom to develop targeted action plans that address identified challenges and capitalize on strengths.

Through these measures, school districts cultivate a culture of continuous improvement that propels educators and students toward greater success. By openly acknowledging areas in need of improvement and actively working to address them, schools demonstrate a commitment to excellence and growth. This commitment inspires confidence among stakeholders and creates an environment where everyone feels valued and supported in their pursuit of educational goals.

Transparent dissemination of survey results and purposeful discussions are potent catalysts for fostering positive transformation. They provide a platform for innovation, collaboration, and shared responsibility, driving ongoing improvements in teaching, learning, and school culture. By embracing transparency and fostering open dialogue, school districts can create a continuous learning and improvement culture that benefits the entire school community.

Upon reflecting on the intricate dynamics of educational practices, it's unmistakable that leveraging surveys is crucial, as underscored by the following recap:

- End-of-year surveys are vital tools for assessing school culture and evaluating leadership effectiveness.
- Surveys capture diverse perspectives from leaders, teachers, students, and parents, providing a comprehensive view of the educational environment.
- Insights from surveys inform targeted strategies to address issues and build upon successes, promoting transparency and collaboration.
- Survey data can predict student achievement, allowing leaders to prioritize interventions and enhance learning outcomes.
- Transparent dissemination of survey results fosters a culture of openness, trust, and collective reflection, driving continuous improvement in educational practices.

The Transformative Impact of Collaborative Mentorship Programs

Discover the transformative power of Collaborative Mentorship Programs, where district-level administrators and local higher education institutions join forces to cultivate the future leaders of education. This strategic alliance, bolstered by robust mentorship initiatives, creates an unparalleled opportunity for emerging leaders to thrive and make a profound impact on educational practices. Through personalized guidance, access to expertise, and a supportive network, mentorship programs empower individuals to grow professionally, fostering a culture of continuous learning and innovation. Embrace the potential of collaborative mentorship to drive meaningful change and shape the trajectory of education for generations to come.

Recognizing the imperative nature of this endeavor, borne from my extensive experience and mentorship of countless aspiring education leaders, I passionately champion the imperative need for a collaborative nexus between district-level administrators and local higher education institutions. This symbiotic partnership stands as the linchpin in cultivating an environment conducive to the flourishing of future leaders, thereby enriching and positively transforming the educational landscape.

At the heart of this collaborative effort lies the recognition of the invaluable role that mentorship programs play in nurturing future leaders. Having personally mentored numerous emerging school leaders throughout my career, I have witnessed firsthand the transformative impact of mentorship on professional growth and leadership development.

School districts can tap into a wealth of resources and expertise by forging partnerships with local higher education institutions offering leadership programs. These institutions often boast faculty members who are experts in educational leadership and are well-equipped to provide valuable insights and guidance to aspiring school leaders.

Mentorship programs facilitated through these partnerships offer emerging leaders the opportunity to benefit from the wisdom and experience of seasoned professionals. Through one-on-one mentorship relationships, emerging school leaders can receive personalized guidance, support, and feedback as they navigate the complexities of educational leadership.

Moreover, mentorship programs provide emerging leaders access to a supportive network of peers and mentors who share similar aspirations and challenges. This sense of community fosters collaboration, shared learning, and mutual support, empowering emerging leaders to overcome obstacles and achieve their full potential.

By investing in mentorship programs, school districts are committed to cultivating a pipeline of effective, visionary leaders who can drive positive change within their schools and communities. Furthermore, mentorship programs help to build a culture of continuous learning and professional growth, ensuring that school leaders remain agile, adaptive, and responsive to the evolving needs of students and educators.

A powerful synergy between district-level administrators and local higher education institutions, bolstered by robust mentorship initiatives, represents a profound strategy for nurturing the next generation of educational trailblazers. Through harnessing the collective wisdom and resources of academia and the school district, we can forge a supportive ecosystem that empowers both novice and emerging leaders to not only thrive but also revolutionize educational methodologies.

Unlocking the transformative power of mentorship programs is essential in molding the future of educational leadership. Here is a recap of the benefits of mentorship:

1. Collaborative Partnership: Take action by forming partnerships between district administrators and local higher education institutions to actively drive positive change in education.
2. Mentorship's Impact: Embrace mentorship programs as powerful tools for personal and professional growth, leveraging firsthand experiences to witness their transformative effects.
3. Access to Expertise: Tap into a wealth of knowledge and resources through partnerships with higher education institutions, empowering educators with insights from experienced faculty in leadership programs.
4. Personalized Guidance: Implement one-on-one mentorship relationships to provide tailored support and feedback, ensuring emerging school leaders receive the individualized guidance they need to succeed.
5. Cultivating Effective Leaders: Make a commitment to cultivating a culture of mentorship and continuous learning, fostering the development of visionary leaders who can drive positive change within schools and communities.

Crafting Comprehensive Professional Development for Leaders

District leaders are pivotal in shaping the professional development landscape for current and aspiring principals within their educational communities. It is imperative that these leaders collectively design and implement comprehensive professional development initiatives tailored to meet the evolving needs of educational leadership.

At the core of these initiatives are regular sessions meticulously crafted to provide principals with ongoing opportunities for growth, reflection, and skill enhancement. These sessions serve as a cornerstone of professional development programs, offering a structured platform for principals to engage in meaningful learning experiences.

District leaders convene regular sessions to ensure that principals remain abreast of the latest research, trends, and best practices in educational leadership and developments in school culture and pedagogy. These sessions provide a forum for principals to delve into effective instructional strategies, data-driven decision-making, student assessment, and fostering inclusive school environments.

Regular professional development sessions allow principals to engage in collaborative learning experiences with their peers. Through facilitated discussions, case studies, and interactive workshops, principals can share insights, exchange ideas, and problem-solve together, drawing upon collective expertise and diverse perspectives.

District leaders should incorporate personalized elements into professional development initiatives in addition to group sessions to address the unique needs and interests of individual principals. This may include opportunities for one-on-one coaching, mentoring, or action research projects tailored to specific leadership goals and areas for growth.

Professional development initiatives should extend beyond traditional workshop formats to encompass experiential learning opportunities. Principals should be encouraged to participate in site visits, job-shadowing experiences, and collaborative projects with other schools or districts, which would provide them with hands-on learning experiences and exposure to innovative practices.

It is essential that professional development initiatives align with the district's broader goals and priorities and the individual needs of principals and their respective schools. By fostering a continuous learning and improvement culture, district leaders can empower principals to lead with confidence, innovation, and effectiveness, ultimately driving positive outcomes for students and educators alike.

In addition to structured professional development sessions, educational practices should incorporate opportunities for principals to engage with real-world scenarios, fostering a dynamic learning environment that directly applies to their leadership roles. These scenarios serve as invaluable learning experiences, allowing principals to immerse themselves in practical situations and gain insights into their leadership styles and the prevailing school culture.

By encountering real-world challenges, principals can identify areas for improvement in their leadership approach and their school's culture. They are prompted to critically reflect on their actions, decisions, and interactions within the school community, enabling them to discern strengths to leverage and areas for growth to address.

These reflective practices are indispensable for principals as they provide the requisite tools to enact impactful strategies to enrich the school culture. Through self-assessment and feedback from peers and mentors, principals can refine their leadership style, adapt their approach to diverse situations, and cultivate a positive and supportive school environment.

Before diving into the specific strategies for professional development, it's crucial to recognize the importance of reflective practices for principals. These practices provide essential tools for implementing impactful strategies that enrich school culture. Through self-assessment and feedback from peers and mentors, principals can refine their leadership style, adapt to diverse situations, and cultivate a positive and supportive school environment. With this understanding, let's explore the key components of effective professional development for school leaders:

- Design Comprehensive Initiatives: Tailored to meet evolving needs of educational leadership, fostering ongoing growth, reflection, and skill enhancement.
- Stay Updated: Ensure principals are informed about latest research, trends, and best practices, covering effective instructional strategies, data-driven decision-making, and fostering inclusive environments.
- Facilitate Collaborative Learning: Engage principals in discussions, case studies, and workshops, encouraging sharing of insights and problem-solving among peers.
- Incorporate Personalized Elements: Offer one-on-one coaching, mentoring, or action research projects, tailoring initiatives to specific leadership goals and growth areas.
- Include Experiential Learning: Encourage participation in site visits, job-shadowing, and collaborative projects, providing hands-on experiences and exposure to innovative practices.
- Align with District Goals: Ensure initiatives align with broader district objectives and individual school needs, fostering a culture of continuous learning and improvement.
- Engage with Real-World Scenarios: Provide opportunities to immerse in practical situations, prompting reflection on leadership styles and school culture for improvement.

Moreover, engaging with real-world scenarios allows principals to test hypotheses, experiment with different strategies, and assess the outcomes of their actions in a controlled yet authentic setting. This experiential learning approach fosters innovation, creativity, and adaptability, qualities essential for effective educational leadership in today's ever-changing landscape.

By participating in real-world scenarios, principals gain a deeper understanding of the complexities and nuances of school leadership. They develop empathy, resilience, and problem-solving skills as they navigate various challenges and dilemmas encountered in their day-to-day roles.

Overall, incorporating opportunities for principals to engage with real-world scenarios enhances the effectiveness of educational practices by providing practical, hands-on experiences that directly impact their leadership development and improve school culture. It empowers principals to lead with confidence, insight, and efficacy, driving positive outcomes for students, educators, and the school community.

Tailored support for school culture is crucially important, especially in urban school districts where the challenges and needs of each school can vary significantly. Recognizing the diverse dynamics within urban settings, it is imperative to provide principals with customized assistance to navigate the intricacies of their school environments effectively.

This tailored support will empower principals to address each school's unique objectives in a targeted and efficient manner. By understanding the specific context, demographics, and challenges their schools face, principals can develop strategies that resonate with their students, staff, and community.

One essential aspect of tailored support is the provision of robust administrative leadership. This involves establishing clear communication channels, setting high expectations, and providing adequate resources to support the school's mission and goals. Strong administrative leadership sets the tone for the school community, fostering a sense of purpose, direction, and accountability.

Targeted professional development initiatives are vital in supporting school culture in urban districts. These initiatives should be designed to address the specific needs and challenges principals and educators face in urban settings. Professional development programs may focus on culturally responsive teaching, equity and inclusion, trauma-informed practices, and community engagement strategies.

Professional development opportunities should be provided at both the district and school levels to ensure alignment with broader educational goals while also addressing the unique needs of individual schools. District-level initiatives can offer resources, expertise, and networking opportunities, while school-level programs can provide more localized support tailored to each school's specific context.

By tailoring support for school culture in urban districts, principals are better equipped to foster a positive and conducive learning environment that meets the diverse needs of their students. This approach not only enhances student outcomes but also promotes a sense of belonging, equity, and community engagement within urban schools. Ultimately, tailored support empowers principals to lead confidently and effectively, driving positive change and transformation within their schools.

Recruitment Strategies for School District HR Departments

The insights derived from my study hold significant value for school districts' HR departments, particularly when selecting new leaders or filling internal vacancies. By leveraging the study's findings, HR departments can make more informed decisions that align with the educational institution's overarching goals and vision.

These insights serve as a guiding light, providing HR departments with valuable information about the leadership qualities and attributes that contribute to a positive school culture and student achievement. By understanding the characteristics of effective leaders, as identified in the study, HR departments can tailor their recruitment and selection processes to identify candidates who possess these desired traits.

Moreover, the study highlights the transformative potential of utilizing diverse data sources in decision-making processes. By incorporating a range of data points, including feedback from stakeholders, performance metrics, and observations, school districts can gain a comprehensive understanding of the factors influencing school culture and student outcomes.

This multifaceted approach to data analysis enables HR departments to make more holistic and evidence-based decisions when hiring new leaders or promoting from within. It also emphasizes the importance of considering qualitative insights alongside quantitative data, ensuring a more nuanced understanding of the leadership landscape within the organization.

Utilizing data-driven decision-making to positively impact school culture and student achievement is crucial. Through the strategic use of data to inform leadership practices and organizational strategies, school districts can pinpoint areas for enhancement, allocate resources efficiently, and deploy targeted interventions to bolster student success.

Ultimately, these insights enable HR departments to embrace a strategic approach to leadership recruitment and development. Through harnessing the transformative potential of data, school districts can foster a culture of excellence, innovation, and continual enhancement, thereby facilitating positive outcomes for students, educators, and the wider school community.

The implementation of the HR selection strategies outlined below reflects a holistic approach to recruitment and development, specifically targeting school leaders. With the overarching goal of driving positive outcomes for both students and educators, these strategies prioritize identifying transformative leaders who align with the institution's goals and vision.

- Structured Interview Process
- Behavioral Assessments
- Staff Input Gathering
- Thorough Reference Checks
- Professional Development Offerings
- Mentorship Programs
- Collaboration and Shared Leadership

Essential Factors for Transformational School Leadership

Transformational school leaders play a pivotal role in shaping the educational landscape, and they must remain cognizant of several key factors to drive positive change and foster a culture of excellence within their schools.

First and foremost, transformational leaders must be aware of their preferred leadership style. Understanding one's leadership style allows leaders to leverage their strengths and adapt their approach to different situations and challenges in the school environment. Whether they lean towards a participative, visionary, or servant leadership style, leaders must continuously reflect on their leadership practices and effectiveness in achieving the desired outcomes.

Additionally, transformational leaders need a clear leadership mission that aligns with the school or district's overall vision and goals. Articulating a compelling mission statement helps provide direction, inspire stakeholders, and rally support for initiatives to improve student outcomes and school culture.

Effective parent involvement is another critical factor that transformational leaders must consider. Engaging parents as partners in education fosters a collaborative relationship between the school and the community, leading to enhanced student success and well-being. Transformational leaders should implement strategies to involve parents in decision-making processes, communicate regularly about their child's progress, and provide opportunities for meaningful involvement in school activities.

Motivating staff is essential for maintaining a positive and productive school climate. Transformational leaders must employ various methods to inspire and empower teachers and staff members, recognize their contributions, and provide opportunities for professional growth and recognition. By fostering a culture of trust, respect, and appreciation, leaders can cultivate a motivated and committed team dedicated to student achievement.

Transformational leaders must meticulously craft comprehensive plans for continuous professional development, ensuring their ongoing growth and effectiveness in driving positive change. Investing in educators' continuous growth and learning is essential for staying abreast of best practices, instructional methodologies, and emerging trends in education. By offering relevant and targeted professional development opportunities, leaders can empower teachers to excel in their roles and drive innovation in teaching and learning.

Transformational leaders must monitor and analyze the academic performance metrics of students within the school. By tracking student achievement data, identifying trends, and addressing areas of need, leaders can make data-informed decisions to improve teaching and learning outcomes. Regularly assessing academic progress allows leaders to tailor instructional strategies, allocate resources effectively, and implement interventions to support struggling students.

In essence, transformational school leaders must remain mindful of these key factors to effectively lead their schools toward excellence. By prioritizing their leadership style, mission, parent involvement, staff motivation, professional development, and academic performance, leaders can create a nurturing and high-performing school environment conducive to student success and holistic development.

Transformational school leaders must remain cognizant of several key factors:

- Their preferred leadership style
- Their leadership mission
- Strategies for parent involvement
- Methods to motivate staff
- Plans for ongoing professional development
- Academic performance metrics of students within the school.

Understanding and incorporating various aspects of educational leadership is fundamental when charting future school goals and objectives. Educational leaders must recognize and integrate critical elements such as leadership style, mission, vision, culture, and other relevant factors to drive meaningful change and improve educational practices.

First and foremost, leaders must deeply comprehend their preferred leadership style and how it aligns with the goals and needs of their school community. Whether they adopt a transformational, instructional, or distributive leadership approach, leaders should leverage their style to inspire and motivate stakeholders, foster collaboration, and facilitate positive change within the school environment.

Equally important is clearly understanding the school's mission, vision, and culture. The mission statement articulates the purpose and values of the school, guiding decision-making and setting the direction for educational initiatives. A compelling vision provides a roadmap for the future, outlining the desired outcomes and aspirations for student success and holistic development. Additionally, understanding the school's culture, including its norms, beliefs, and traditions, is essential for creating an environment where all members feel valued, respected, and supported.

Exceptional leaders can consider all these factors comprehensively, setting themselves apart through their holistic approach to leadership. By integrating leadership style, mission, vision, and culture into their practices, leaders can cultivate an influential school culture characterized by trust, collaboration, and a shared commitment to excellence. They can effectively communicate the school's goals and values, engage stakeholders in meaningful dialogue, and align efforts toward common objectives.

Furthermore, leaders can leverage their understanding of these aspects to foster innovation, promote equity and inclusivity, and address the diverse needs of their school community. They can create professional growth and development opportunities, build strong relationships with students, staff, parents, and community partners, and lead by example through their actions and decisions.

In essence, by comprehensively considering these critical aspects of educational leadership, leaders can set a solid foundation for continuous improvement and success. They can navigate challenges, seize opportunities, and inspire positive change, ultimately impacting the lives of students and the broader school community.

Catalysts of Change

Driving cultural change within schools is a profound endeavor that begins with individual leaders who lead with purpose and vision. These leaders serve as catalysts, igniting a transformation in school culture to achieve collective success. Drawing from extensive research and insightful interviews with school leaders, it becomes evident that the essence of education lies not only in academic excellence but also in fostering a positive school culture through effective leadership.

Effective leaders understand that school culture is the heartbeat of the educational environment, influencing every aspect of the teaching and learning process. They recognize the importance of creating a nurturing, inclusive, and supportive culture where all school community members feel valued, respected, and empowered to thrive.

Through purposeful leadership, these individuals inspire and motivate others to embrace change, challenge the status quo, and work collaboratively towards shared goals. They embody their values and principles, modeling integrity, empathy, and a commitment to continuous improvement.

Effective leaders leverage research-based strategies and best practices to inform their approach to cultural transformation. They invest time and effort in understanding their school community's unique needs and dynamics, tailoring their leadership style and initiatives accordingly.

By fostering a positive school culture, these leaders create an environment where students feel safe, engaged, and motivated to learn. They cultivate a sense of belonging and connection, fostering relationships built on trust and mutual respect.

Furthermore, effective leaders prioritize ongoing communication and collaboration, involving all stakeholders in decision-making and seeking input from diverse perspectives. They encourage open dialogue, active participation, and feedback, recognizing that meaningful change requires collective effort and buy-in from the school community.

In essence, driving cultural change within schools requires visionary leadership informed by research and grounded in a deep understanding of the importance of school culture. By leading with purpose, integrity, and empathy, individual leaders can inspire a transformation that enhances academic outcomes and enriches the overall educational experience for students, educators, and families alike.

Transformational leaders in education are not merely administrators but creators of an environment where students and educators thrive. They understand that the school is not just a physical, educational space but a dynamic ecosystem shaped by every member and influencing every individual. Therefore, leaders are responsible for nurturing this ecosystem's positive and growth-oriented culture.

These leaders celebrate collaboration among teachers, recognizing teamwork is essential for fostering innovation and achieving common goals. They empower educators by giving them the autonomy and support they need to excel in their roles, fostering a sense of ownership and investment in the school's mission.

Educational leaders understand the importance of remaining adaptable in the ever-evolving educational landscape. They embrace change as an opportunity for growth and transformation, championing innovation and experimentation in teaching and learning practices. By fostering a culture of lifelong learning throughout the school community, they instill in students and educators alike a love for knowledge and a commitment to continuous improvement.

These leaders also recognize the importance of promoting resilience among students, equipping them with the skills and mindset needed to navigate future challenges confidently. They provide a supportive environment where students feel safe taking risks, learning from failure, and persevering in adversity.

Leaders in education play a multifaceted role in shaping the school environment. They cultivate a positive culture of collaboration, empowerment, and innovation while remaining adaptable and fostering lifelong learning. This creates an environment where students and educators can thrive and reach their full potential.

Transformative leadership in education goes beyond mere management; it's a commitment to cultivating a school culture that transcends mediocrity. It involves creating an environment where curiosity is encouraged, diversity is celebrated, and every individual feels valued and supported.

The influence of transformative leaders extends far beyond their words; it's reflected in their actions and decisions, setting the tone for the entire school community. They inspire growth and innovation, leaving a lasting legacy of inspiration and progress.

But transformative leadership is not just a theoretical concept—it's a call to action. As you turn the final pages of this book, let its insights catalyze your journey toward building and sustaining a vibrant school culture. By embracing transformative leadership principles, you have the power to shape the future of education and society.

In our journey together, we embark on a collaborative quest, bound by our dedication to crafting educational environments where every student not only survives but thrives. This voyage is dedicated to unlocking the full potential of educators, nurturing a culture where they can truly excel in their roles, and fostering communities that flourish as a result.

Our path begins with the acknowledgment of the paramount importance of school culture. We understand that it serves as the cornerstone of the educational experience, influencing every facet of teaching and learning. Thus, we commit ourselves to creating environments that are nurturing, inclusive, and supportive, where every member of the school community feels valued and empowered. Key strategies to achieve this include:

- Recognizing school culture as crucial
- Creating nurturing, inclusive, and supportive environments
- Inspiring and motivating others towards shared goals
- Modeling integrity, empathy, and continuous improvement
- Tailoring leadership style to unique school dynamics

As we traverse this transformative journey, we aspire to inspire and motivate others towards shared goals, modeling integrity, empathy, and a commitment to continuous improvement. We recognize the need to tailor our leadership style to the unique dynamics of each school, fostering safety, engagement, and motivation in our students, and cultivating a sense of belonging and trust through meaningful relationships. Further strategies to implement include:

- Fostering safety, engagement, and motivation in students
- Cultivating belonging and trust through relationships
- Prioritizing communication and collaboration

- Involving stakeholders in decision-making
- Encouraging open dialogue and feedback

Communication and collaboration stand as pillars of our approach, as we prioritize involving stakeholders in decision-making, encouraging open dialogue, and celebrating collaboration among teachers. We instill a culture of lifelong learning, promoting resilience among students and nurturing a positive environment of collaboration, empowerment, and innovation. Additional strategies to embrace include:

- Celebrating collaboration among teachers
- Instilling a culture of lifelong learning
- Promoting resilience among students
- Cultivating a positive culture of collaboration, empowerment, and innovation

Our leadership is not merely theoretical but manifested in action, reflecting transformative principles and inspiring growth. Together, we collaborate towards the shared goal of crafting vibrant educational environments where every individual can thrive and contribute to the collective flourishing of our communities.

A Journey of Educational Empowerment

In this journey, we recognize the inherent value and potential within each student, understanding that they deserve environments that nurture their growth, inspire their curiosity, and cultivate their unique talents. We strive to create classrooms and schools where learners feel valued, supported, and motivated to achieve their highest aspirations.

We acknowledge educators' pivotal role in shaping the future. By providing them with the necessary support, resources, and professional development opportunities, we empower them to unleash their creativity, innovation, and passion for teaching. In doing so, we create spaces where educators can thrive personally and professionally, leading to enriched learning experiences for their students.

But our journey extends beyond the walls of individual schools—it encompasses entire communities. By fostering strong partnerships between schools, families, and community stakeholders, we create environments where everyone is invested in the success and well-being of our learners. Together, we build networks of support, collaboration, and shared responsibility, ensuring that every child has the opportunity to reach their full potential.

So, let us embark on this journey with a shared vision of educational excellence, equity, and inclusivity. By working collaboratively, we can create learning environments where every student can thrive, every educator can excel, and every community can flourish.

Now is the moment to embrace your calling as a visionary leader and recognize your profound influence in shaping the educational landscape. Authentic leadership serves as the catalyst for transformative change, fostering a culture where every individual—be it students, educators, or community members—can truly thrive.

As you embark on this journey, remember that the power to effect change lies within your hands. By embodying the principles of authentic leadership and integrating the wisdom gleaned from these pages into your practice, you become an agent of positive transformation within your educational community.

Embrace your unique role as a leader and recognize the ripple effect of your actions. Your decisions, values, and commitment to excellence set the tone for the entire educational environment. Through your leadership, you can inspire others, cultivate innovation, and create a culture of empowerment and growth.

But let's not forget, the path to educational excellence commences with you. As you navigate the forthcoming challenges and opportunities, uphold your vision, stay resolute in your commitment to authenticity, and lead with compassion and integrity.

Your journey as a visionary leader isn't solitary; it's a collaborative effort that demands dedication and unwavering determination. Together, we have the power to shape a future where every individual can fulfill their potential, and where education serves as a beacon of hope and inspiration.

May our leadership be the catalyst that sparks a wave of positive change, leaving a lasting legacy of empowerment and enlightenment for all involved in the educational journey. As a united front, driven by our shared dedication to shaping the future of education and society, we nurture empowered leaders along the way.

As we embark into unknown territories, let our combined endeavors pave the path for a more inclusive and equitable educational landscape. Let's champion innovation, foster resilience, and instill a culture of lifelong learning that enables individuals to thrive in a rapidly evolving world.

With every stride, may we inspire others to join us on this journey of growth and exploration. Together, let's challenge conventions, dismantle barriers, and forge connections that bridge diverse perspectives and experiences.

As we navigate the complexities of educational practice, may our shared vision guide us, our passion fuel us, and our unwavering commitment propel us forward. Together, let us leave an indelible mark on the fabric of education, shaping a future where every learner has the opportunity to flourish and succeed.

May your leadership, inspired by the transformative essence of creating and sustaining a thriving school culture, serve as a beacon of hope and inspiration, lighting the path for future generations of educators, learners, and leaders. Let us seize this moment to redefine what is possible and create a world where education is a transformative force for good. Let's embark on this journey together, recognizing that leadership starts with each of us, as we shape the future of education and society—one empowered leader at a time.

Notes

Workbook - Chapter Four - The Evolution of Leadership Style

This workbook section for Chapter Four empowers educational leaders to reflect deeply on their evolving leadership styles and enact intentional changes that foster positivity within their school communities. It provides actionable steps for leaders to amplify their influence and inspire future generations. May your leadership, infused with the transformative essence of creating and sustaining a thriving school culture, serve as a beacon of hope and inspiration, guiding educators, learners, and leaders toward a future where education is a catalyst for profound societal change. Together, let's redefine possibilities and cultivate a world where education stands as a transformative force for good, shaping a brighter future for all. These practical steps are essential for leaders to incorporate into their daily practice, ensuring continual growth and impact.

Assessing the Influence of Leadership Styles

- *Question 1:* To what extent do you believe the leadership styles implemented in your district have influenced the cultivation of either a positive or negative school culture?

____

____

____

____

- *Reflection:* Reflect on the various leadership styles in your district and their impact on school culture.

____

____

____

____

- *Action Step:* Evaluate the leadership styles in your district by listing two examples of positive and two examples of negative influences they have had on the school culture. Propose actions to reinforce the positive and mitigate the negative influences.

____

____

____

____

Correlating Leadership Styles with Staff and Student Outcomes

- *Question 2:* How do you assess the correlation between leadership styles and the morale, engagement, and performance of staff and students within your schools?

____

____

____

____

- *Reflection:* Consider how different leadership styles affect the overall morale and performance of both staff and students.

____

____

____

____

- *Action Step:* Design a survey or feedback tool to gather data on staff and student morale, engagement, and performance related to leadership styles. Analyze the results to identify patterns and correlations. Develop a plan to address any issues and promote positive outcomes.

____

____

____

____

Impact of Leadership on Trust and Collaboration

- *Question 3:* In what ways do you think the leadership styles exhibited by school administrators impact the level of trust and collaboration among teachers, students, and parents?

____

____

____

____

- *Reflection:* Reflect on the role of leadership in building trust and fostering collaboration within the school community.

- *Action Step:* Identify three leadership behaviors that have either strengthened or weakened trust and collaboration in your school. Create an action plan to enhance behaviors that build trust and collaboration, including specific activities or initiatives to be implemented.

Inspirational Leadership for Future Generations

- *Reflection:* Reflect on how your leadership, inspired by the transformative essence of creating and sustaining a thriving school culture, can serve as a beacon of hope and inspiration for future generations.

- *Action Step:* Write a personal vision statement that captures your commitment to being an empowered leader who inspires others. Include specific goals and actions you will take to lead by example and influence positive change in education.

____

____

____

____

Summary of Chapter Four Insights

- *Reflection:* Summarize your key insights and takeaways from Chapter Four in a concise paragraph.

____

____

____

____

- *Action Step:* Identify one new strategy related to the evolution of leadership styles that you will implement based on what you have learned in this chapter. Describe how you will measure its effectiveness and the impact it aims to achieve.

____

____

____

____

Final Reflection and Commitment

- *Reflection:* Reflect on the entire journey through the workbook and your growth as a transformative leader.

____

____

____

____

- *Action Step:* Commit to one long-term goal that embodies the principles of transformative leadership. Outline a detailed action plan to achieve this goal, including milestones, resources needed, and methods for measuring progress.

____

____

____

____

GLOSSARY OF TERMS

four framework. An approach created by Bolman and Deal to determine the leadership type leaders fall into.

human resource framework. Leaders who support, advocate, and empower others.

leadership style. The traits, behaviors, and characteristic methods of a person in a leadership position.

organizational structure. Determines how roles, power, responsibilities, and information flow are delegated, controlled, and coordinated within a leadership hierarchy.

parental involvement. The participation of parents in school activities.

political framework. Leaders who advocate, focusing on coalition and building.

Priority school. One that has been identified as one of the lowest-performing 5 percent of Title 1 schools in the state over the past three years or any non-Title 1 school that would otherwise meet the same criteria.

professional development. The process of improving and increasing the capabilities of staff through education and training opportunities.

Renew school. One that is considered to have a strong leader, excellent teachers, a building with flexible resources, and is engaged with and supports families and students.

school culture. The shared beliefs and priorities that drive the thinking and actions of people within a school community.

staff motivation. Activities within an organization or through a supervisor that aim to reaffirm the importance of staff members' jobs and to improve their skills, motivation, and qualifications.

structural framework. Leaders who focus on analysis and design with a focus on structure, strategy, environment, implementation, experimentation, and adaptation.

student discipline. Goals that ensure the safety of staff and students, creating an environment conducive to learning.

symbolic framework. Leaders who inspire others, view organizations as stages, use symbols to capture attention and provide interpretations of experiences.

BIBLIOGRAPHY

Andrews, Richard L., and Roger Soder. "Principal Leadership and Student Achievement." *Educational Leadership* 44 no. 6 (March 1987): 9–11.

Baker, Bruce D., Danielle Farrie, and David Sciarra. *Is School Funding Fair? A National Report Card*. Seventh Edition: February 2018. Rutgers University, Education Law Center.

Barr, BA. "A Study of the Impact of Leadership on Secondary School Culture." Unpublished doctoral dissertation. Minneapolis: Capella University, 2006.

Blase, Joseph. and Peggy Kirby. *Bringing out the Best in Teachers: What Successful Principals Do.* Thousand Oaks, CA: Corwin Press, 2000.

Bolman, Lee and Terrence Deal. *Reframing Organizations: Artistry, Choice, and Leadership.* Hoboken, NJ: Jossey-Bass Publishers, 1991, and Thousand Oaks, CA: Corwin Press, 2003.

"Leading with Soul and Spirit." *School Administrator* 59, no. 2 (February 2002): 21–6. https://eric.ed.gov/?id=EJ640834.

Bohte, J. "Examining the Impact of Charter Schools on Performance in Traditional Public Schools." *PSJ* 32, no. 4 (November 2004): 501–20. doi: 10.1111/j.1541-0072.2004.00078.x.

Bredeson, PV and Brad Kose. "Responding to the Education Reform Agenda: A Study of School Superintendents' Instructional Leadership." *Education Policy Analysis Archives* 15 (March 2007): 5. doi: 10.14507/epaa.v15n5.2007.

Bryan, J. "Fostering Educational Resilience and Achievement in Urban Schools through School-Family Community Partnerships."

Professional School Counseling 8, no. 3 (February 2005): 219–27. https://www.jstor.org/stable/i40102889.

Chung, Jae Young, In-Soo Shin, and Heesook Lee. The Effectiveness of Charter School: Synthesizing Standardized Mean-Changes. *KEDI Journal of Educational Policy* 6, no. 1 (2009): 61–80.

Coleman, James S., E Campbell, C Hobson, F McPartland, A Mood, et al. "Equality of Educational Opportunity." Washington, DC: US Government Printing Office, 1966.

Coleman, James S. and Thomas Hoffer. *Public and Private High Schools: The Impact of Communities.* New York: Basic Books, 1987.

de Wolf, Inge F. and Frans Janssens. "Effects and Side Effects of Inspections and Accountability in Education: An Overview of Empirical Studies." *Oxford Review of Education* 33, no. 3 (2007): 379–96.

Deal, Terrence, Kennedy, Allan, & Kennedy, Allan A. (1982). *Corporate Cultures: The Rites and Rituals of Organizational Life* (pp. 98–103). Reading, Mass: Addison-Wesley.

Deal, Terrence, & Peterson, Kent. (1990). *The Principal's Role in Shaping School Culture*. Washington, DC: US Government Printing Office.

Shaping School Culture: The Heart of Leadership. Hoboken, NJ: Jossey-Bass, 1999.

Dinham, Stephen. (2005). "Principal Leadership for Outstanding Educational Outcomes." *JEA* 43, no. 4 (December 2004): 338–56. https://www.emerald.com/insight/publication/issn/0957-8234.

Dorner, Lisa, James Spillane, and James Pustejovsky. "Organizing for Instruction: A Comparative study of Public, Charter, and Catholic Schools." *J Educ Change* 12 no. 1 (October 1, 2010): 71–98. doi: 10.1007/s10833-010-9147-5.

Dressler, Boyd. "Charter School Leadership." *Education and Urban Society* 33, no. 2 (Feb 2001): 170–85. doi: 10.1177/0013124501332006.

DuFour, Richard and Robert Marzano. "High-Leverage Strategies for Principal Leadership." *Educational Leadership* 66, no. 5 (February 2009): 62–8.

Ediger, Marlow. "Improving the School Culture." *Education* 118, no. 1 (fall 1997): 36.

Elmore, Richard. "Accountability and Capacity" in *The New Accountability: High Schools and High-Stakes Testing*, Martin Carnoy, Richard Elmore, and Leslie Siskin, eds. New York: Routledge, 2003, 195–209.

"Accountable Leadership." *The Educational Forum* 69, no. 2 (January 2008): 134–42. doi: 10.1080/00131720508984677.

Fullan, Michael. "Principals As Leaders in a Culture of Change." *Educational Leadership* 59, no. 8 (special issue May 2002): 16–21.

"The Role of Leadership in the Promotion of Knowledge Management in Schools." *Teachers and Teaching* 8, no. 3 (August 2002): 409–19. doi: 10.1080/13540600210000530.

Gawlik, Marytza. "Breaking Loose: Principal Autonomy in Charter and Public Schools." *Educational Policy* 22, no. 6 (September 2007): 783–804. doi: 10.1177/08959048073070.

Goldman, Elise. "The Significance of Leadership Style." *Educational Leadership* 55, no. 7 (April 1998): 20–22.

Goleman, D. (2000). "Leadership that gets results." *Harvard Business Review*, March 2000..

Gonder, PO and D Hymes. "Improving School Culture." AASA Critical Issues, report no. 27. American Association of School Administrators, 1801 N. Moore Street, Arlington, VA 22209 (Stock No. 21-00393), 1994.

Guskey, Thomas R. "Closing the Knowledge Gap on Effective Professional Development." *Educational Horizons* 87, no. 4 (2009): 224–33.

Hallinger, Philip. "Leading Educational Change: Reflections on the Practice of Instructional and Transformational Leadership." *Cambridge Journal of Education* 33, no. 3 (2003): 329–52. doi 10.1080/0305764032000122005.

Hamilton, Laura, Richard Halverson, Sharnell Jackson, Ellen Mandinach, Jonathan Supovitz, et al. "Using Student Achievement Data to Support Instructional Decision-Making." *Scholarly*

Commons (September 2009). https://repository.upenn.edu/handle/20.500.14332/35036.

Hersey, Paul and Kenneth Blanchard. *Management of Organizational Behavior: Leading Human Resources.* Englewood Cliffs, NJ: Prentice-Hall, 1993.

Hersey, Paul. *Management of Organizational Behavior: Leading Human Resources*. Prentice Hall, 2001.

Hess, Frederick and Andrew Kelly. "Learning to Lead? What Gets Taught in Principal Preparation Programs." *Teachers College Record* 109, no. 1 (2007): 244–74. doi: 10.1177/016146810710900105.

Hickey, Wesley and Sandra Harris. "Improved Professional Development through Teacher Leadership." *Rural Educator* 26, no. 2 (2005): 12–16.

Hill, Paul and Josephine Bonan. "Site-Based Management: Decentralization and Accountability." *Education Digest* 57, no. 1 (1991): 23.

Hollander, EP. "Leadership and Decision-Making" (book review). *Administrative Science Quarterly* 18, no. 4 (1993): 556–8.

Howard, WC. "Leadership: Four Styles." *Education* 126, no. 2 (2005): 384–91.

Hoy, Wayne K., C Tarter, and R Kottkamp. *Open Schools/Healthy Schools: Measuring Organizational Climate.* Thousand Oaks, CA: Corwin Press/Sage Publications, 1991.

Hoy, Wayne K. and Dennis Sabo. *Quality Middle Schools: Open and Healthy.* Thousand Oaks, CA: Corwin Press, 1998.

Jordan, Debra. *Leadership in Leisure Services: Making a Difference.* Andover, MA: Venture Publishing, 1996.

King, M. Bruce and Fred Newmann. "Building School Capacity through Professional Development: Conceptual and Empirical Considerations." *International Journal of Educational Management,* 15, no. 2 (April 2001): 86–94.

Kelley, Robert, Bill Thornton, and Richard Daugherty. "Relationships between Measures of Leadership and School Culture." *Education* 126, no. 1 (2005): 17.

Kullar, P. A multisite case study: "The effect of principal leadership on school culture and student achievement in charter schools in Los Angeles, California" (doctoral dissertation), 2011. Retrieved from https://www.proquest.com/openview/aded283ac8602d54e1deb3df5ab21ddc/1?pq-origsite=gscholar&cbl=18750

Kurland, Hanna, Hilla Peretz, and Rachel Hertz-Lazarowitz. "Leadership Style and Organizational Learning: The Mediate Effect of School Vision." *Journal of Educational Administration* 48, no. 1 (2010): 7–30.

Lazaridou, Angeliki. "Values in Principals' Thinking When Solving Problems." *International Journal of Leadership in Education* 10, no. 4 (2007): 339–56.

Leithwood, Kenneth and Mary Poplin. "The Move toward Transformational Leadership." *Educational Leadership* 49, no. 5 (1992): 8–12.

Leithwood, Kenneth and Carolyn Riehl. *What We Know about Successful School Leadership*. Nottingham: National College for School Leadership, 2003. https://olms.ctejhu.org/data/ck/file/What_we_know_about_SchoolLeadership.pdf

Olson, Lynn. "Quality Counts '99 To Track Accountability in States." December 16, 1998.

Linn, Robert, Eva Baker, and Damian Betebenner. "Accountability Systems: Implications of Requirements of the No Child Left Behind Act of 2001." *Educational Researcher* 31, no. 6 (2002): 3–16. doi: 10.3102/0013189X031006003.

MacNeil, Angus, Doris Prater, and Steve Busch. "The Effects of School Culture and Culture on Student Achievement." *International Journal of Leadership in Education* 12, no. 1 (2009): 73–84.

Malen, Betty and Jennifer Rice. "A Framework for Assessing the Impact of Education Reforms on School Capacity: Insights from Studies of High-Stakes Accountability Initiatives." *Educational Policy* 18, no. 5 (2004): 631–60.

Marzano, Robert, Timothy Waters, and Brian McNulty. "School Leadership That Works: From Research to Results." *Association for Supervision and Curriculum Development* (2005).

Meindl, James. "The Romance of Leadership As a Follower-Centric Theory: A Social Constructionist Approach." *The Leadership Quarterly* 6, no. 3 (1995): 329–41.

Mintzberg, Henry. *Mintzberg on Management: Inside Our Strange World of Organizations*. New York: Simon and Schuster, 1989.

Murphy, Joseph, Jost Yff, and Neil Shipman. "Implementation of the interstate school leaders licensure consortium standards." *International Journal of Leadership in Education* 3, no. 1 (Jan-March 2000): 17–39.

National Center for Education Statistics. (2022). Explore Results for the 2022 NAEP Reading Assessment. Retrieved from https://nces.ed.gov/nationsreportcard/reading/results/

Natriello, Gary. Review of *Public and Private High Schools: The Impact of Communities. The American Sociologist* 18, no. 3 (fall 1987): 296–299. http://www.jstor.org/stable/27702571.

Northouse, Peter. *Leadership: Theory and Practice*. Thousand Oaks, CA: Sage Publications, 2015.

Oshagbemi, Titus and Samuel Ocholi. "Leadership Styles and Behavior Profiles of Managers." *Journal of Management Development* 25, no. 8 (2006): 748–62.

Pashiardis, Petros. "Group Decision Making: The Role of the Principal." *International Journal of Educational Management* 7, no. 2 (1993). doi: 10.1108/09513549310026921.

Pepper, Kaye and Lisa Thomas. "Making a Change: The Effects of the Leadership Role on School Culture." *Learning Environments Research* 5, no. 2 (2002): 155–66.

Pepper, Kaye. "Effective Principals Skillfully Balance Leadership Styles to Facilitate Student Success: A Focus for the Reauthorization of ESEA." *Planning and Changing* 41, no. 1/2 (2010): 42–56.

Peterson, Kent and Terrence Deal. "How Leaders Influence the Culture of Schools." *Educational Leadership* 56, no. 1 (Sept. 1998): 28–31.

Popham, W. James. *The Truth about Testing: An Educator's Call to Action*. ASCD.org, 2001.

Quinn, DM. “The Impact of Principal Leadership Behaviors on Instructional Practice and Student Engagement.” *Journal of educational administration* 40, no. 5 (2002): 447–467.

Ravitch, Diane. “Why I Changed My Mind.” The Nation, June 14, 2010.

Roach, Andrew and Thomas Kratochwill. “Evaluating School Climate and School Culture.” *Teaching Exceptional Children* 37, no. 1 (2004): 10–17. doi: 10.1177/004005990403700101.

Roby, David. “Teacher Leaders Impacting School Culture.” *Education*, vol. 131, no. 4, p. 782. (Year of publication not provided).

Şahin, S. “The Relationship between Instructional Leadership Style and School Culture (İzmir Case).” *Educational Sciences: Theory and Practice* 11, no. 4 (2011): 1920–27.

Please add the date published and authors’ first names.

Sanders, M. and A Harvey. “Beyond the School Walls: A Case Study of Principal Leadership for School-Community Collaboration.” *The Teachers College Record* 104, no. 7 (2002): 1345–68.

Sarason, S. “Commentary: Leadership and Charter Schools.” *International Journal of Leadership in Education* 2, no. 4 (1999): 379–81.

Sashkin, Marshall, and Herbert J. Walberg, eds. Educational Leadership and School Culture. Institute of Education Sciences. ERIC Number: ED367056, 1993, 195 pages. ISBN: ISBN-0-8211-1861-7.

Schechter, C. and M Qadach. “Toward an Organizational Model of Change in Elementary Schools: The Contribution of Organizational Learning Mechanisms.” *Educational Administration Quarterly* 48, no. 1 (2012): 116–53.

Sergiovanni, TJ. *Leadership: What’s in It for Schools?* London: Psychology Press, 2001.

Shaw, BC. “Impact of Leadership Styles on School Culture” (doctoral dissertation). Capella University, 2009.

Spillane, James, Tim Hallett, and John Diamond. “Forms of Capital and the Construction of Leadership: Instructional Leadership in Urban Elementary Schools.” *Sociology of Education* 76, no. 1 (Jan. 2003): 1–17.

Stewart, Jan. "Transformational Leadership: An Evolving Concept Examined through the Works of Burns, Bass, Avolio, and Leithwood." *Canadian Journal of Educational Administration and Policy* 54 (June 2006): 1–29.

Sullivan, Susan and Jeffrey Glanz. *Building Effective Learning Communities: Strategies for Leadership, Learning, and Collaboration.* Thousand Oaks, CA: Corwin Press, 2006.

Tondeur, Jo, Geert Devos, Mieke Van Houtte, Johan van Braak, and Martin Valcke. "Understanding Structural and Cultural School Characteristics in Relation to Educational Change: The Case of ICT Integration." *Educational Studies* 35, no. 2 (April 2009): 223–35. doi: 10.1080/03055690902804349.

Ubben, Gerald, Larry Hughes, and Cynthia Norris. *The Principal: Creative Leadership for Excellence in Schools.* New York: Pearson, 2015.

Useem, Elizabeth. "Learning from Philadelphia's School Reform: The Impact of NCLB and Related State Legislation." Final draft of revised book chapter. May 8, 2006.

Vroom, Victor and Philip Yetton. *Leadership and Decision-Making.* Pittsburgh, PA: University of Pittsburgh Press, 1973.

Wagner, Christopher and Penelope Masden-Copas. "An Audit of the Culture Starts with Two Handy Words." *Journal of Staff Development* 23, no. 3 (2002): 42–53.

Webb, LD and M Norton. *Human Resources Administration: Personnel Issues and Needs in Education.* Upper Saddle River, NJ: Prentice Hall, 2003.

Whitaker, Todd. *What Great Principals Do Differently: 18 Things That Matter Most.* London, UK: Routledge, 2011.

_______. *What Great Teachers Do Differently: 17 Things That Matter Most.* London, UK: Routledge, 2012.

Woods, P. *Democratic Leadership in Education.* London: Sage, 2005.

Wren, D. "School Culture: Exploring the Hidden Curriculum." *Adolescence* 34, no. 135 (1999): 593.

ABOUT THE AUTHOR

Dr. Shana Burnett's journey in education is a testament to her unwavering dedication to her community and passion for transformative leadership. Beginning her illustrious career as a teacher in her hometown of Newark, New Jersey, Dr. Burnett consciously chose to invest her talents where they mattered most – in the school district that shaped her upbringing. For over 25 years, she remained a steadfast pillar, raising her family in the vibrant city she loved.

Dr. Burnett wore many hats throughout her tenure, each contributing to her wealth of experience and deep-rooted understanding of educational dynamics. From school aide to principal, she navigated diverse roles within the Newark Public School District, immersing herself in the intricate tapestry of school cultures and leadership styles.

Amidst this diverse educational landscape, Dr. Burnett's fervent dedication to transformational leadership emerged. Motivated by her rich experiences, she embarked on rigorous research during her doctoral studies, exploring innovative approaches to improving educational outcomes by examining the correlation between leadership styles and school culture.

Dr. Burnett's commitment to student achievement transcended conventional boundaries, extending beyond the confines of the classroom. One tangible manifestation of her advocacy was the creation of the Urban Professional Development event – a dynamic platform meticulously crafted to foster both personal and professional growth within the community.

Dr. Burnett's impact transcends the boundaries of her immediate surroundings. She has championed excellence in public education through grant writing, committee service, and educational publications, leaving an indelible mark on the field. As a beacon of inspiration and advocacy, Dr. Shana Burnett stands as a shining example of the profound difference one individual can make in the lives of many.

TRANSFORMATIVE LEADERSHIP

CREATING AND SUSTAINING A THRIVING SCHOOL CULTURE

WORKBOOK

Chapter One - School History

This workbook section for Chapter One is designed to help educational leaders reflect deeply on their contributions, deliberate actions, and understanding of school reforms. My goal is to encourage you to take practical steps that drive positive changes in your educational communities. By thoughtfully considering these aspects, you can better shape a thriving school culture and make a lasting impact on students, educators, and the wider community.

Shaping Educational History Through Leadership

- *Question 1:* How does your leadership contribute to shaping the history of education within your school district?

____

____

____

____

- *Reflection:* Reflect on your leadership journey and how your initiatives have influenced the educational landscape.

____

____

____

____

- *Action Step:* Document two key initiatives or programs you have led that have made a significant impact on your school district. Describe the outcomes and how they have shaped the district's educational history.

____

____

____

____

Instigating Profound Changes in School Culture

- *Question 2:* What deliberate actions are you taking to instigate profound changes in the school culture that leave a lasting impact on students, educators, and the wider community?

____

____

____

____

- *Reflection:* Consider the strategies and actions you have implemented to drive cultural change.

____

____

____

____

- *Action Step:* Develop a detailed plan outlining three specific actions you are taking to transform your school's culture. Include timelines, expected outcomes, and methods for evaluating success. Ensure these actions are sustainable and leave a lasting legacy.

____

____

____

____

Understanding and Implementing School Reforms

- *Question 3:* What is your understanding of school reforms and the belief that they should be connected to a school's unique culture for the school community to thrive?

____

____

____

____

- *Reflection:* Reflect on your knowledge of school reforms and their significance in your school's context.

- *Action Step:* Write a brief essay (300-500 words) on the importance of aligning school reforms with the unique culture of your school. Provide examples from your experience where this alignment has led to positive outcomes. Discuss the challenges and benefits of this approach.

Summary of Chapter One Insights

- *Reflection:* Summarize your key insights and takeaways from Chapter One in a concise paragraph.

- *Action Step:* Identify one new strategy you will implement based on what you have learned in this chapter. Describe how you will measure its effectiveness and the impact it aims to achieve.

____

____

____

____

Chapter Two - Exploring Leadership Styles and Their Impact

This workbook section for Chapter Two emphasizes the crucial role of understanding your leadership style as the foremost action step for educational leaders. It guides you in reflecting on your leadership approach and taking deliberate actions to foster a positive and inclusive environment within your schools. By recognizing how your leadership style influences school culture and the well-being of students, educators, and the wider community, you can personalize and expand upon these exercises to effectively meet the specific needs of your school community.

Understanding and Reflecting on Leadership Styles

- *Question 1:* How does your awareness of your leadership style influence the culture within your school community?

____

____

____

____

- *Reflection:* Think about how your leadership style is perceived by others and how it impacts the school culture.

____

____

____

____

- *Action Step:* Identify your leadership style and list three ways it has positively or negatively influenced your school community. Reflect on how this awareness shapes your interactions and decisions.

___

___

___

___

Fostering a Positive and Inclusive Environment

- *Question 2:* What deliberate actions are you taking to ensure that your leadership style fosters a positive and inclusive environment for all stakeholders?

___

___

___

___

- *Reflection:* Consider the strategies you employ to create an inclusive atmosphere where everyone feels valued.

___

___

___

___

- *Action Step:* Develop a plan that includes three specific actions you are currently taking or plan to take to promote inclusivity. Outline the steps, timelines, and methods for evaluating the effectiveness of these actions.

____

____

____

____

Leadership Style Assessment

- *Reflection:* Complete a self-assessment of your leadership style using a provided leadership style inventory on page 165. Reflect on the results and how they align with your self-perception.

____

____

____

____

- *Action Step:* Based on your assessment results, identify one area for growth. Create a personal development plan with steps to enhance this aspect of your leadership style.

____

____

____

____

Case Study Analysis

- *Reflection:* Read a case study about a school leader who successfully transformed their school culture. Reflect on the leadership style demonstrated and its impact on the school community.

____

____

____

____

- *Action Step:* Write a summary of the case study and compare it to your own leadership experiences. Identify two strategies used in the case study that you can implement in your context.

____

____

____

____

Summary of Chapter Two Insights

- *Reflection:* Summarize your key insights and takeaways from Chapter Two in a paragraph.

____

____

____

____

- *Action Step:* Identify one new strategy related to your leadership style that you will implement based on what you have learned in this chapter. Describe how you will measure its effectiveness.

____

____

____

____

Chapter Three - Historical Overview

This workbook section for Chapter Three is crafted to assist educational leaders in introspecting on their roles and actions concerning understanding historical contexts, cultivating school culture, involving parents, motivating staff, and supporting professional development. It encourages practical steps to amplify their leadership impact and foster a positive educational environment.

Understanding the Historical Context of Education

- *Question 1:* What role do you think school leaders play in comprehending the historical overview of education?

____

____

____

____

- *Reflection:* Reflect on the importance of understanding the history of education in your leadership role.

____

____

____

____

- *Action Step:* Research and write a summary of a significant historical event in education. Discuss how this event has influenced current educational practices and how it informs your leadership approach.

____

____

____

____

Cultivating School Culture

- *Question 2:* Do you believe school leaders must cultivate the culture of a school to conform with the distinct school community as a means of attaining achievement?

____

____

____

____

- *Reflection:* Consider the relationship between school culture and the unique characteristics of the school community.

____

____

____

____

- *Action Step:* Outline three specific strategies you use or plan to use to align your school's culture with its community. Include steps to implement these strategies and ways to measure their success.

____

____

____

____

Parental Involvement in Schools

- *Question 3:* How much do you believe parental involvement plays in the daily functioning of running a school?

____

____

____

____

- *Reflection:* Reflect on the role of parents in the school community and their impact on school operations.

____

____

____

____

- *Action Step:* List two examples of effective parental involvement initiatives you have implemented or observed. Describe the outcomes and how these initiatives contributed to the school's success.

Motivating Staff

- *Question 4:* What role do you think school leaders play in motivating their staff?

- *Reflection:* Think about how your leadership can inspire and motivate your staff.

- *Action Step:* Identify three motivational strategies you use or plan to use to boost staff morale. Detail how you will implement these strategies and track their effectiveness.

Involvement in Professional Development

- *Question 5:* How much do you think school leaders should be involved in the professional development of their staff?

- *Reflection:* Reflect on the importance of professional development and your role in facilitating it.

- *Action Step:* Develop a professional development plan for your staff. Include specific training sessions, workshops, or other opportunities, and describe how you will support and encourage staff participation.

Outline methods for evaluating the impact of these professional development activities.

___

Summary of Chapter Three Insights

- *Reflection:* Summarize your key insights and takeaways from Chapter Three in a concise paragraph.

- *Action Step:* Identify one new strategy related to the historical overview, school culture, parental involvement, staff motivation, or professional development that you will implement based on what you have learned in this chapter. Describe how you will measure its effectiveness and the impact it aims to achieve.

Chapter Four - The Evolution of Leadership Style

This workbook section for Chapter Four empowers educational leaders to reflect deeply on their evolving leadership styles and enact intentional changes that foster positivity within their school communities. It provides actionable steps for leaders to amplify their influence and inspire future generations. May your leadership, infused with the transformative essence of creating and sustaining a thriving school culture, serve as a beacon of hope and inspiration, guiding educators, learners, and leaders toward a future where education is a catalyst for profound societal change. Together, let's redefine possibilities and cultivate a world where education stands as a transformative force for good, shaping a brighter future for all. These practical steps are essential for leaders to incorporate into their daily practice, ensuring continual growth and impact.

Assessing the Influence of Leadership Styles

- *Question 1:* To what extent do you believe the leadership styles implemented in your district have influenced the cultivation of either a positive or negative school culture?

____

____

____

____

- *Reflection:* Reflect on the various leadership styles in your district and their impact on school culture.

____

- *Action Step:* Evaluate the leadership styles in your district by listing two examples of positive and two examples of negative influences they have had on the school culture. Propose actions to reinforce the positive and mitigate the negative influences.

Correlating Leadership Styles with Staff and Student Outcomes

- *Question 2:* How do you assess the correlation between leadership styles and the morale, engagement, and performance of staff and students within your schools?

- *Reflection:* Consider how different leadership styles affect the overall morale and performance of both staff and students.

- *Action Step:* Design a survey or feedback tool to gather data on staff and student morale, engagement, and performance related to leadership styles. Analyze the results to identify patterns and correlations. Develop a plan to address any issues and promote positive outcomes.

Impact of Leadership on Trust and Collaboration

- *Question 3:* In what ways do you think the leadership styles exhibited by school administrators impact the level of trust and collaboration among teachers, students, and parents?

- *Reflection:* Reflect on the role of leadership in building trust and fostering collaboration within the school community.

- *Action Step:* Identify three leadership behaviors that have either strengthened or weakened trust and collaboration in your school. Create an action plan to enhance behaviors that build trust and collaboration, including specific activities or initiatives to be implemented.

Inspirational Leadership for Future Generations

- *Reflection:* Reflect on how your leadership, inspired by the transformative essence of creating and sustaining a thriving school culture, can serve as a beacon of hope and inspiration for future generations.

- *Action Step:* Write a personal vision statement that captures your commitment to being an empowered leader who inspires others. Include specific goals and actions you will take to lead by example and influence positive change in education.

____

____

Summary of Chapter Four Insights

- *Reflection:* Summarize your key insights and takeaways from Chapter Four in a concise paragraph.

____

____

____

____

- *Action Step:* Identify one new strategy related to the evolution of leadership styles that you will implement based on what you have learned in this chapter. Describe how you will measure its effectiveness and the impact it aims to achieve.

____

____

____

____

Final Reflection and Commitment

- *Reflection:* Reflect on the entire journey through the workbook and your growth as a transformative leader.

____

____

- *Action Step:* Commit to one long-term goal that embodies the principles of transformative leadership. Outline a detailed action plan to achieve this goal, including milestones, resources needed, and methods for measuring progress.

Leadership Style Assessment

Use the following leadership style inventory to identify your dominant leadership style.

Instructions:

1. Respond to each statement based on your natural tendencies in a leadership role.
2. Use the following scale to rate each statement:
   - 1 = Strongly Disagree
   - 2 = Disagree
   - 3 = Neutral
   - 4 = Agree
   - 5 = Strongly Agree

Statements:

Leadership Style #1

1. I often create a compelling vision of the future. ______
2. I am able to inspire others to share in my vision. ______
3. I encourage innovative thinking and new ideas. ______

Leadership Style #2

4. I seek input from team members before making decisions. ______
5. I promote open communication and collaboration within my team. ______
6. I value the opinions and suggestions of others. ______

Leadership Style #3

7. I challenge my team to achieve their best potential. ______
8. I emphasize the importance of personal development and growth. ______
9. I lead by example and set high standards for performance. ______

Leadership Style #4

10. I use rewards and punishments to motivate my team. ______
11. I set clear goals and expectations for team members. ______
12. I monitor performance closely and provide corrective feedback when necessary. ______

Leadership Style #5

13. I prefer to make decisions without consulting others. ______
14. I expect my team to follow my directives without question. ______
15. I maintain strict control over all aspects of the work process. ______

Leadership Style #6

16. I give my team members a lot of freedom to do their work. ______
17. I provide minimal supervision and let my team make their own decisions. ______
18. I believe in delegating tasks and responsibilities to team members. ______

Leadership Style #7

19. I prioritize the needs of my team above my own. ______
20. I seek to serve others and help them grow and succeed. ______
21. I focus on building strong relationships and a sense of community within my team. ______

Leadership Style #8

22. I use my charisma to influence and inspire others. ______
23. I am confident and articulate in presenting my ideas. ______
24. I am able to build strong emotional connections with my team members. ______

How to Interpret Your Scores:

- High Scores: A high score in a particular leadership style indicates that you naturally exhibit traits associated with that style. Consider how you can leverage these strengths in your leadership role.

- Moderate Scores: A moderate score suggests that while you may exhibit some traits of this leadership style, it is not your dominant style. You can work on developing these traits further if they align with your leadership goals.
- Low Scores: A low score indicates that this is not a natural leadership style for you. It may be beneficial to focus on your dominant styles while being aware of the potential areas for growth.

Leadership Style Assessment Results

Thank you for completing the Leadership Style Assessment. Below you will find the interpretation of your scores. Each score represents your tendency towards a particular leadership style based on your responses. The highest scores indicate your predominant leadership styles.

1. Visionary Leadership: Visionary leaders are known for their ability to create a compelling vision of the future and inspire others to share in that vision. They encourage innovative thinking and are adept at motivating their team towards long-term goals.
    - Your Score
2. Democratic Leadership: Democratic leaders seek input from team members before making decisions. They promote open communication and value the opinions and suggestions of others, fostering a collaborative team environment.
    - Your Score
3. Transformational Leadership: Transformational leaders challenge their team to achieve their best potential. They emphasize personal development and growth, leading by example and setting high standards for performance.
    - Your Score
4. Transactional Leadership: Transactional leaders use rewards and punishments to motivate their team. They set clear goals and expectations, closely monitor performance, and provide corrective feedback when necessary.
    - Your Score

5. Autocratic Leadership: Autocratic leaders prefer to make decisions without consulting others. They expect their team to follow directives without question and maintain strict control over all aspects of the work process.
    - Your Score
6. Laissez-Faire Leadership: Laissez-faire leaders give their team members a lot of freedom to do their work. They provide minimal supervision and allow the team to make their own decisions, delegating tasks and responsibilities.
    - Your Score
7. Servant Leadership: Servant leaders prioritize the needs of their team above their own. They seek to serve others, help them grow and succeed, and focus on building strong relationships and a sense of community within the team.
    - Your Score
8. Charismatic Leadership: Charismatic leaders use their charisma to influence and inspire others. They are confident and articulate in presenting their ideas and are able to build strong emotional connections with their team members.
    - Your Score

Remember, effective leadership often involves adapting your style to fit the needs of your team and the situation. Use this assessment as a tool for self-awareness and professional development.

By using this inventory, you can gain valuable insights into your leadership styles and develop strategies to lead more effectively.

Reference

If you use or reference this inventory in your work, please cite it as follows:

Dr. Shana Burnett, "Transformative Leadership: Creating and Sustaining a Thriving School Culture", InnovateEd Solutions, 2024

Printed in the United States
by Baker & Taylor Publisher Services